PRIVILEGES AND PITFALLS

The Life of J K Stephen

PRIVILEGES AND PITFALLS

The Life of J K Stephen

D J Leighton

HYDRANGEA
PUBLISHING

First published in the United Kingdom in 2009 by
Hydrangea Publishing
6 Walnut Tree Cottages, London SW19 5DN

A catalogue record for this book is available from the British Library.
ISBN 978-0-9548495-2-8

Printed by Intype Libra, Elm Grove, Wimbledon SW19 4HE
Typeset by GR Typesetting, Cambridge, UK.

Front Cover:

i   An oil painting of J. K. Stephen by Charles Wellington Furse dated 1891.
   (By kind permission of The Provost and Scholars of King's College,
   Cambridge).

ii Quotation from 'Portraits' by Desmond MacCarthy

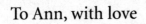

To Ann, with love

D. J. Leighton was educated at King's College School, Wimbledon and later at Christ's Hospital. On leaving school he became a salesman with Unilever, and later spent time in advertising and the Middle East. He is now retired, and lives in Wimbledon with his wife Ann.

His previous books include 'Montague Druitt. Portrait of a Contender' and 'J. K. Stephen. The Collected Works of a Victorian Poet'.

He is a member of the Poetry Society and the Chelsea Arts Club.

Contents

Acknowledgements

A great many people have helped me put this book together, and I am most grateful to them all. In particular I should like to thank:

Maria Bossley, Gary A. Brown, John Carter, Pamela Clark, Steve Collier, Nicky Colman, Tony Connor, Susan Cornelius, Steve Dingvean, Patricia Edge, Elizabeth Ennion, Robert Fyson, Penny Hatfield, Guy Holborn, Michael Johnson, Sean Kirwan, Prakesh Makwana, Julian Malone-Lee, David and Pamela McCleave, James McDermott, Patricia McGuire, Dr David Munday, Peter Nicholls, Andy & Sue Parlour, Elaine Quigley, Robert Smith, Charlotte Villiers, Fiona Woodfield and Nick Woodward.

I would also like to acknowledge the cooperation of all the individuals and organisations who have allowed me to use their material and photographs. I also thank Trinity College, Cambridge for giving me access to Harry Wilson's diary. If there are any inadvertent omissions I apologise, and these will be corrected in later editions.

D. J. Leighton

Illustrations

Preface

On Friday 5 February 1892, a sad, brief notice appeared in The Times newspaper announcing the death of one James Kenneth Stephen. It's simplicity marked the passing of a man who had surely been destined for fame and success at the highest levels. Stephen was 32 years old and he died in St Andrew's Lunatic Asylum, Northampton.

In at least three arenas Stephen seemed likely to bestride the period covering the late 19th and early 20th centuries. The author and poet A C Benson thought that parliament would have had to reduce the minimum age for judges to accommodate Stephen's legal prowess. Many of his friends from Eton and Cambridge believed he was of prime minister material, and the Times Literary Supplement, never a journal to exaggerate a talent, in a tribute fifty years after his death, bracketed him with the very best 19th century poets of light verse including Winthrop Praed, Charles Calverley, and Thomas Hood. Further, he was selected by the Prince of Wales, with the approval of Queen Victoria, to tutor the Prince's eldest son and second in line to the throne, Prince Albert Victor, for entrance into Cambridge. Later Albert Victor became better known as Prince Edward (Eddy) and the Duke of Clarence.

It is surprising for a man of such gifts and promise, that no dedicated biography has been written and so little attempt made to understand why Stephen did not sustain the terms 'brilliant' and 'genius' that were so often applied to him. Instead he crashed to earth like some burnt out meteor, his reputation spoilt by madness and innuendo. On the 150th anniversary of his birth, this book seeks to deliver the story of James Kenneth Stephen, so that he may take up the corner of history that he deserves.

Chapter 1

Early Days

With a lineage that can be traced back to the 17th century
French aristocracy, a father who was a senior High Court judge
and an aunt who was the daughter of the poet William
Makepeace Thackeray, it might be assumed that James
Stephen's predecessors had a long history of social and
professional success. In fact, for the previous two hundred years
his family had had to battle from obscurity and even disrepute.

In the mid 1700s the family, led by James Stephen of
Ardenbraught, had been traders and smugglers in Scotland.
Stephen had seven sons and one of them, William, set up a
lucrative slave trade business from the West Indies. Another
son, James, became a merchant. One night he was returning
from the South of France with a cargo of wine when a storm
blew up and he was shipwrecked off the coast of Dorset. To
protect his cargo from plunder, he quickly became friends with
a Mr Milner, the local excise officer, and even moved in as his
lodger. The officer soon rued his generosity as Stephen eloped
with, and secretly married, his daughter, Sibella. Soon he was
in more trouble when his trading business failed and he found
himself in heavy debt and on route to the King's Bench gaol. In
prison he articulately and disruptively argued his case which
although it did not secure his quick release, encouraged him
to write a pamphlet 'Considerations on Imprisonment for
Debt'. He quoted the Magna Carta to show that sending

debtors to prison was foolish and illegal. On release, he tried to set up as a solicitor but his reputation went before him and the Benchers at the Inns of Court rejected him, because of his 'want of birth, want of fortune, want of education and want of temper'.

It was James Kenneth Stephen's great grandfather, another James, who guided the family into calmer waters. He began as an 'evidence collector' and helped in Sir Fowell Buxton's enquiry into the slave trade. From this he developed a campaign against slavery and worked with William Wilberforce for its abolition. Wilberforce's daughter, Sarah, became his second wife. He was also elected an MP and achieved the rank of Master in Chancery. This ambition and ability to climb the social ladder manifested itself in subsequent Stephen generations.

James Kenneth Stephen was born on 25 February 1859 at 15 Sunderland Terrace in West London. No 15 was, and remains, a five storey early Victorian terraced house in a small tree-lined side street in the middle of Bayswater. His parents were James and Mary Stephen, and his father became better known as Sir James Fitzjames Stephen. At the time of Stephen's birth his legal career was in full swing. He had been called to the Bar at the Inner Temple in January 1854 and eighteen months later he joined the Midland Circuit on the advice of its leader Kenneth Macaulay. It was to mark this friendship with Macaulay that Sir James named his son after him and invited him to become his godfather. This was duly accepted and Stephen was christened James Kenneth. Sir James's work on the Midland Circuit took him away from London so much of the time that the young Stephen saw little of his father. The ambition, which was beginning to characterise the Stephen dynasty showed itself again in 1865 when Sir James stood for parliament in the general election as the Progressive Parliamentary Candidate for Harwich. He failed but was warmly commended for his efforts. Some years later Benjamin Disraeli wrote in a letter to Lord Lytton 'It is a thousand pities that J F Stephen is a judge; he might have done anything and everything as a leader of the future Conservative party'. Probably though, it is just as well a political career was nipped in the bud in view of the later difficulties he encountered.

Stephen saw even less of his father when in 1869 Sir James was appointed the legal member of the Indian Viceroy's council on the recommendation of Henry Maine, the retiring holder of the post. The opportunity to follow in the steps of Macaulay and Maine, and to play a key part in shaping the legal system in India was too good to turn down so in November 1869 he left for India where he remained until April 1872. On the journey out to Bombay, Sir James filled his time by writing twenty articles for the Pall Mall Gazette. His wife, Mary, visited him twice in India and each time took Rosamund their youngest daughter, who was still an infant. It was during a visit to Simla that another daughter Dorothea was born. Rosamund also accompanied her father on a tour of the West of Ireland. Stephen never saw his father in India and indeed Sir James preferred the family to be brought up at home as he had little interest in small children. However he did ensure that their lives were happy and that they were well looked after.

Despite the absence of his father for long periods it does not seem that during his childhood, Stephen ever developed a relationship with his mother. She appeared to cause him emotional upsets and tantrums. As a result he tried to stay aloof of her, and allowed her into his life as little as possible. Little is known about her, save that before marriage she was

Mary Richenda Cunningham, the daughter of a clergyman. By reputation she was rather cold, stern and dominated by her husband and her religious beliefs. Her father had been the editor of the Christian Observer. Stephen never saw her as a source of advice and the detachment remained for the rest of his life. Of greater influence on Stephen's upbringing were the expectations put on him and his siblings. His father's friends who came to the house were all highly ambitious and there was an expectation to succeed in whatever challenge, usually intellectual, presented itself. Bad behaviour was not tolerated, and so Stephen learnt to keep his feelings under control for as long as he could. In all Stephen had nine brothers and sisters. A brother and sister Leslie and Margaret, died in infancy and another sister, Frances died of rheumatic fever in 1880. James Stephen was the middle of the three brothers. Herbert was born in 1857 and Henry three years later. Both became barristers. The family was completed by the four sisters, Katherine, the oldest child, then Helen, Rosamund and Dorothea.

Up to the age of eight Stephen had been educated at home but then his parents sent him to board at Park House School in Southborough near Tonbridge in Kent. The Mathieson's Trade Directory for 1867-8 describes it as a 'gentlemen's school'. Also in the town were two similar schools: William Farmcombe's School at Hapsburg House and Miss Taylor's Preparatory School. Park House School was run by the Rev. W C Wheeler who had moved to the area two years earlier. The school catered for boys 8 – 13 and several of them had their roots elsewhere in the Empire, such as the East Indies. The school provided a general education that took in French, mathematics, classics, and religious studies, plus English, history and geography. There were six domestic staff, all women, including a cook, housemaids and general servants. A contemporary photograph of the school shows it to be in a very substantial house with a large garden in which a game of cricket is in progress. The dress of the boys suggests they met the description of 'young gentlemen'.

It must have been the plan for Stephen to stay several years at Park House before moving on to a public school, but his father was keen to do his utmost to ensure that that school was Eton. This preference was a little surprising in view of his own unhappy time there. Sir James had been constantly bullied because of his studious manner and his dislike of games, which he viewed as childish and of 'absurd importance'. He lacked the courage to retaliate. He said himself 'I was on the whole very unhappy at Eton and I deserved it; for I was shy, timid and I must say cowardly'. He also believed the teaching at Eton 'to be wretched' and the classes far too large. In mitigation he liked the fact that 'the boys were gentlemen by birth and breeding' and that there was 'an absence of moral or religious enthusiasm' due to the mechanical dullness of the chapel services. On the day that Sir James left Eton he tore off his white tie and stamped it into the mud. His abiding conviction from Eton was that 'the process taught me for life the lesson that to be weak is to be wretched, that the state of nature is a state of war'. Sir James's father had noted his son's unhappiness and finally allowed him to leave the school early, aged 16, and to complete his pre-university education at King's College, London. Here he flourished amongst more purposeful colleagues and he achieved a good level of academic success. He went on to Trinity College, Cambridge in 1847.

Despite these opinions of Eton, Sir James determined that it was still the only suitable school for the son of a socially ambitious barrister with aspirations to be a High Court Judge. He also realised that an Eton education would almost guarantee his son the opportunity of a fine career somewhere in the imperial dominions. Perhaps after twenty years he had had time to come to terms with, or indeed forget, his experiences. Maybe he was the embodiment of his brother Leslie's view that bullying would not cease until men stopped 'dwelling more fondly upon their school days in proportion to the remoteness of their memories'. At any rate when Stephen was nine, after one year at Park House, Sir James contacted an old friend who was a master at Eton. His name was Oscar Browning. Browning's advice, far from disinterested, was that James's path to Eton would be more certain if he transferred to another boarding school at Thorpe Mandeville in Buckinghamshire, which so happened to be owned by Browning's brother, the Rev. W T Browning. Oscar Browning's motive became even less praiseworthy when it is realised that although the school was certainly a recognised route into Eton, Browning was a career homosexual who used to visit his brother's school and cherry-pick those pupils that he fancied seeing at Eton. Leslie Stephen noted in a book about Sir James, that young Stephen 'gave promise of unusual strength and a combination of power and sweetness in his features'.

Thorpe Mandeville School was a conversion of the Old Manor House carried out in 1853. Always a huge building (it had garrisoned Cromwell's troops in 1664) with massive grounds and several ponds, it became even bigger as a school with several extensions drawn up by the county architect George Clark. The school took in about 30 pupils, all of whom were boarders. The Reverend Browning became headmaster in 1854 and remained in charge until the school closed in the mid-1880s. Stephen stayed at Thorpe Mandeville under the watchful eyes of the Browning brothers until he was twelve and then true to expectations and Oscar Browning's plans, was elected a Colleger at Eton in second from top place.

Unlike his father, who had lived in a private house in Windsor to protect him from 'the obscure sins that afflicted the boarders', Stephen was plunged into College. Many of the upper classes and public school headmasters, such as the Rev. William Dobson of Cheltenham College were ambivalent towards these 'obscure sins'. William Stead, a leading editor, said a few years later 'Should everyone found guilty of Oscar Wilde's crime be imprisoned, there would be a very surprising emigration from Eton, Harrow, Rugby and Winchester to the jails of Pentonville and Holloway'. It was into this bearpit of immorality that Stephen was asked to take his chance.

Chapter 2

The Makings of a Legend

'Despite its lack of movement, the Wall Game is very tiring indeed and ruthlessly tough. There is nothing frivolous about the rule which forbids you actually gouge out an opponent's eye, whilst on muddy days an appeal for air from the depths of the bully is as sacred as an SOS at sea' – 'Eton: How it Works' by JDR McConnell.

Even today, more than 130 years later, James Stephen's heroic feats in the Eton Wall Game are remembered and celebrated in an annual toast. The particular event which gave rise to this ceremony occurred in 1876 in the match between the Collegers and the Oppidans. Stephen was captain and 'Keeper of the Wall' for the former and for some reason the rest of his side were late for the start. The game had to begin with Stephen alone facing eleven Oppidans. Somehow he secured the ball, and withstanding all the brutal attempts of the Oppidans, held it for fifteen minutes until his team-mates appeared. The Collegers then went on to win the game by four 'shies' to none and so brought to an end a long series of drawn matches. The incident quickly moved into legend and Stephen became a hero who embodied the myth of College superiority. AJ Ayer recalls in his book 'Memoirs of a Philosopher' how Stephen is remembered. 'After the Wall Game the College eleven used to assemble in Hall and drink a loving cup 'in piam memoriam JKS' ('in pious memory'). The ceremony continues to this day much as Ayer described it. The game takes place on or about 30 November, and at the end of the supper afterwards, the toast is drunk by the Collegers. Some hundred years later the ebullient Conservative MP and now Mayor of London Boris Johnson followed in Stephen's footsteps. He too was 'Keeper of the Wall' and captain of the Collegers. Johnson's style was described as 'like an echidna[1] on heat'. A ditty composed after his third and last appearance ran 'Hey, hey ABJ how many Oppidans did you kill today?' Even for Johnson there were limits. Asked if he had ever bitten an opponent, he replied 'No, no, I wasn't a biter'. Stephen would have been delighted that his baton had been passed on so honourably.

Stephen was tough and determined, so to take up the Wall Game was natural. He first got into the team in 1874, aged 15, which was remarkably young, and then remained in the side until he left Eton. For the last two years, 1876 and 1877 he was 'Keeper of the Wall' and in both years the Collegers had convincing victories. He was further honoured as Keeper of the Mixed Wall. This meant the captain of the best players in a unified Collegers and Oppidans team. This positioned him as the outstanding player in the school. Stephen played the game in plimsoles and tradition still maintains that he was the best 'furker'[2] Eton has ever seen. Such was his enthusiasm for the game that when his Eton days were over he continued for the next ten years to take a team to play the Collegers. These were certainly not light-hearted encounters. Oliver Chandos, an Etonian and aristocrat described them as follows 'Matches between boys and 'old boys' were especially violent, different generations seeking to justify themselves'. Nevertheless Stephen

---

[1] A vicious spine covered animal with long claws.
[2] A player who moves or passes the ball backwards.

loved the game and described it as 'for a game played there which most who've tried it declare it is a truly noble game'. Years later when he had become established as a writer of light verse, he alluded nostalgically to memories of the Wall Game.

> 'There were two good fellows I used to know,
> How distant it all appears!
> We played together in football weather
> And messed together for years
> Now one of them's wed, and the other's dead
> So long that he's hardly missed
> Save by us, who messed with him years ago
> But we're all in the Old School list'

Both his friends can be identified. In the fifth line 'one of them's wed' was Henry Chester Goodhart, a formidable Wall player who excelled in the 1876 match. A report describes his contribution 'two shies quickly obtained by Goodhart, who all through played a fine game' and 'the Collegers again got two shies, one if not both again the work of Goodhart'. Goodhart was also an excellent cricketer and for three seasons played in the Eton XI. He, like Stephen, became a member of the Cambridge Apostles and friend of the Duke of Clarence. Later he was appointed Professor of Latin at Edinburgh University. He died in 1895, aged 37. The other friend in the poem, also mentioned in the fifth line as 'dead' was probably James Wilson who played for the Collegers in the Wall Game with Stephen for three years 1874-6. The two were very close. He went up to King's College, Cambridge a year before Stephen, but died when he was hit by a railway engine on the line at Taplow in Berkshire in the spring of 1879. The other possibility is that the friend was Robert Edmund Pashley who played for the Collegers in 1874 and 1875. He was therefore a team-mate of Stephen and Wilson.

In a poem titled 'The Literary and Scientific Society' that appeared in the Etonian in December 1885, Stephen refers to him. Pashley was its president and Stephen describes him as 'eloquent'. He was the son of a QC, an accomplished modern linguist and on leaving Eton, went to Trinity College, Cambridge. He died there in September 1878 aged 21.

Throughout Stephen's time at Eton, and later at Cambridge, he gravitated towards organizations that usually involved debate or literature. He was especially active in the Eton Society, which served as the school's debating chamber. In his last year and as a member of the prestigious group 'Pop', Stephen opposed the motion that 'the system of education at Eton is satisfactory'. The boy proposing the motion was George Curzon. He enthused 'how vulgar or diffident boys were turned by Eton education into polished gentlemen'. He talked of how 'old Eton men cling to the memory of their school', and their debt of gratitude to Eton. He finished an emotional, if unspecific, speech by referring to the 'interests of the great nation to which we have the honour to belong'. Curzon sounded like a serious politician in the making. Stephen replied that he disliked the manner of teaching and claimed that the use of classroom time at Eton was flawed. He was particularly unhappy with the emphasis on athletics. This was an echo of his father's view and of the intellectual opinion of some of the senior masters, although not of the headmaster, John Hornby. Stephen's speech made particular points rather than relying on the hubris of his opponent, but he lost the motion. Yet he did himself no harm by his articulate attack. Soon after in another debate, Stephen proposed the motion that the reign of William III had been more beneficial to England that that of Louis XIV to France. Again Curzon led the opposite view, but this time Stephen prevailed.

Although Curzon was at this stage no more than a very bright schoolboy, it was a coup that Stephen had defeated in serious debate, someone who would later become Viceroy of India, foreign secretary, and was only denied the premiership by Stanley Baldwin. No wonder colleagues saw in Stephen, the possibility of a real political career. George Curzon was from one of the most aristocratic families in the land. Its lineage could be traced back to William the Conqueror; his father was the 1st Lord Scarsdale, and the family seat was an 820 acre estate at Kedleston Hall. At the time Curzon had collected more prizes at Eton than any other boy in its history, and still found time to captain the Oppidans. Even amongst the boys of Eton, Curzon was perceived as being rather special, and this grandeur was enhanced during his time at Oxford. The Masque of Balliol (Curzon's college) contained this verse:

> 'My name is George Nathaniel Curzon,
> I am a most superior person,
> My cheek is pink, my hair is sleek,
> I dine at Blenheim once a week'.

The composers were JW Mackail who won an Order of Merit for his contribution to scholarship, and Cecil Spring-Rice, whose brother later proposed Stephen for membership to the Savile Club. It was Cecil Spring-Rice who wrote Last Poem, which contained the stirring lines 'I vow to thee my country – all earthly things above – Entire and whole and perfect, the service of my love'. Later he was knighted and became British Ambassador to Washington during the First World War.

Stephen could debate on almost any subject. He could handle the straightforward issues and the academically obscure. For example he put forward a most learned comparison of the merits of Aristophanes and Euripides – a Greek comic poet versus the tragedian playwright, who both pre-dated Christ by about 400 years. In another debate, on the Crusades, Stephen 'considered it a sign of great moral improvement that such wicked and abominable institutions no longer exist'. The value of these debates, especially those involving Stephen, Curzon and Cecil Spring-Rice was that they were genuine discussions, motivated not by some vain intellectualism but by a real wish to explore issues.

The Literary Society to which Stephen belonged but with less recorded effect, was founded by his mentor Oscar Browning. In November 1877 Stephen's father came down to the Literary Society and delivered a comprehensive history of 'the English in India'. The school library was packed and the speech was rapturously received. Amongst the audience was George Curzon. Some twenty years later, now the Viceroy of India, Curzon let it be known in a speech in Derby, that his inspiration to serve in India had been a direct result of Sir James's address. Curzon recalled the occasion:

'Sir James Stephen came down to Eton and told the boys that listened to him, of whom I was one, that there was in the Asian continent an empire more populous, more amazing and more beneficent that that of Rome; that the rulers of that great dominion were drawn from the likes of our own people; that some of them might perhaps in the future be taken from the ranks of the boys who were listening to his words. Ever since that day, and still more since my first visit to India in 1887, the fascination and, if I may say so, the sacredness of India have grown upon me, until I have come to think that it is the highest honour that can be placed upon any subject of the Queen that in any capacity, high or low, he should devote such energies as he may possess to its service'.

It would have been Stephen's influence that persuaded his father to speak at the Literary Society, so some of the impetus for Curzon's meteoric career through India and his promotion to an iconic empire figure came very much from the Stephen family.

Oscar Browning also formed his own Debating Society. He wanted his house to become the centre of intellectual life at the school in order to balance up the shift to sporting priorities. John Hornby, Eton's headmaster, disapproved of these societies, and they became a factor in the eventual breakdown in relationships between the two men, which led to Browning's dismissal.

'Pop', 'that self-perpetuating oligarchy', was a privileged club of senior boys and prefects to which membership was every boy's ambition. It implied brains, seniority and a talent either for public speaking or sport. It allowed members various dress privileges such as wearing waistcoats. Other 'benefits' included the right to carry a cane, to turn down overcoat collars, and to walk on a particular side of the street. It also had its own debating society, and this was probably its most interesting and useful feature. Stephen was elected into 'Pop' and was a regular debater.

Stephen had a hand in at least five newspapers or magazines whilst at Eton. One paper was the Etonian. It was started on 19 May 1875 by Arthur Sandbach and Henry St Clair Feilden. In a sense it was a revival of a paper of the same name that had run in 1821-2, and aimed to put its emphasis on literature, poetry and prose. In 1876 George Curzon became the editor and his most active contributors were Stephen and Cecil Spring-Rice. Stephen's first published poetry appeared in the Etonian on 7 October 1875. It was called 'Lines to the Statue in School Yard'. The following year the Etonian printed several more of Stephen's poems including 'Lines at the Riverside', 'Early School', 'the Critics Speech', and 'Written at Private'. This was a substantial output and evidence of a burgeoning talent. Unfortunately Curzon could not make the magazine pay its way, and with debts of £2 7s and 7d (£2.38p), it came out for the last time on 2 August 1876. Curzon also published a small volume of verse and prose called 'Out of School at Eton' to which Stephen contributed. On this he made a £3 profit, but when Curzon gave up the Etonian this publication faded as well.

The Eton College Chronicle had begun in the early 1860s and placed all its emphasis on sporting events of one sort or another. For example, Stephen found in the College library, a very old Greek poem 'The Hurdles and Quarter of a Mile', which he translated. The Academy journal said of this work, 'those who read his Homeric parody must have prophesied no ordinary career after such a tour de force'. It was published in the Chronicle in 1877.

Another magazine for which Stephen wrote albeit after he had gone up to Cambridge, was the Eton Rambler. Even its founder AC Benson described it as 'short lived and very pretentious'. Stephen sent in several little contributions, amongst them a poem called 'Midsummer', but his feistiest verse was written in indignation at being kept waiting by Benson for a reply to a previous letter:

> 'What means this silence? Is't a seemly thing
> Thus to provoke a friendly elder's ire?
> Take notice then, that if thou answerest not,
> A second letter follows close on this
> Third close on second, fourth as close on third,
> And angry postcards rain as thick as hail
> That slew Egyptia's cattle'

Two other papers which were amongst Stephen's first attempts at journalism were the Salt Hill Papers and the Sugar

Loaf Papers. The first, in which he was helped by Herbert Ryle had one issue dated 4 June 1875. In the second Stephen was again aided by Ryle and Meaburn Tatham. It came out in 1875 as well, and was no more successful.

Stephen's strength and competitive spirit suited him well for his other sporting activity at Eton, rowing. By sheer vigour he contributed much to a boat's performance, but he was little interested in learning the technicalities of the sport, which would have harnessed this power to better effect. The 1876 List of Boats records that he rowed in the Defiance, which was classified amongst the Lower Boats. The following year Stephen moved up to the Upper Boats in the 10-oar Monarch. Because of this recognisable, if not outstanding ability he was known as a 'wet-bob'. There was a less formal occasion when he was rowing in a sweepstake event with his friend Arthur (AC) Benson. Suddenly Stephen started to swing his oars wildly, sending up great waves of water. The boat was a low built gig with high rowlocks, known as a 'cedar' and it soon became flooded and began to sink. Stephen was unperturbed and continued to row as the boat gradually went down. Then at the last minute with the water up to his chin, he abandoned the boat and his friend, and swam for the shore. Benson lived to tell the tale. This incident may have summed up Stephen's attitude to rowing. He saw it as a bit of fun where he could utilise brute force to achieve a degree of amusement.

Throughout Stephen's seven years at Eton, James John Hornby was the headmaster. It was the same Hornby who became involved in a dramatic and prolonged struggle with Oscar Browning, who of course had guided Stephen into his house. This may have split Stephen's loyalties, although in the circumstances he would probably have sided with Browning. Hornby was always likely to be a controversial choice as headmaster, and a schism amongst the senior staff was almost unavoidable. He was an old Etonian, but he had previously been second master at Winchester College. Eton had never before brought in a headmaster from outside, so his appointment marked a new era in the history of the school. He quickly made several changes. French and science became compulsory, and he paid £2000 for a chemistry faculty out of his own pocket. It comprised of a laboratory and lecture room, and was built in brick. The architect was William Wilkinson of Oxford, who as instructed in his brief, made sure that 'provision is made for effectually carrying off the gases occasioned by chemicals'. Morning service became compulsory as well and Hornby started an army corps to prepare boys for Sandhurst. The internal politics of the common room meant that the masters teaching classics disliked their traditional supremacy being eroded by the introduction of new subjects. Hornby had always been keen on games. He played cricket for Eton, rowed for Oxford in the Boat Races of 1849 and 1850, and was a enthusiastic member of the Alpine Club. He now, as headmaster encouraged sport, a policy that did not go down well with the traditionalists amongst the staff. He was rightly described as 'a sort of muscular Christian'. One such member was Oscar Browning, who objected to the changes in academic emphasis and the growing importance of games. By the time of Hornby's appointment in 1868, Browning had been at Eton eight years, long enough for his modus operandi to become, for him, a way of life. In his opinion close personal relationships with particular boys of his choice was the best way to build a happy house and achieve academic success. Such was his renowned favouritism and reputation for 'irrepressible attention' that the need for euphemisms evaporates – he was a paedophile.

One of the first boys who caught Browning's eye at Eton was Charles Dunmore. He became the Seventh Earl of Dunmore when he was four years old. It was early in the 1860s that Browning lamented 'A half or two ago I saw a boy named Dunmore. I was struck by his eyes. I have been more so by his manner and everything about him. My wishes, my hopes and fears begin and terminate in him. I have found that he is a lord, but I loved him before. I never shall have a chance of knowing him, perhaps not one of speaking to him'. Dunmore had no need to worry about Browning. He became a lord-in-waiting to Queen Victoria and later Lord Lieutenant of Stirlingshire, where he owned 80,000 acres. His son Viscount Fincastle, a war correspondence, won the Victoria Cross at Nawah Kili during the Victorian colonial war in India.

Hornby had felt uneasy for a long time about Browning and one or two of the other masters whose loyalty he clearly did not have, because of their teaching methods, and for their lack of morality, as Hornby saw it. He was at last, in 1875, prompted into action when another Eton housemaster, Charles Wolley-Dod, reported to him that Browning was showing 'undue friendliness' to one of Wolley-Dod's boarders. This boy was none other than George Curzon. There had been an apathy bordering on hostility between Curzon and Wolley-Dod, his housemaster from the beginning. The Rev. Charles Wolley-Dod, known as Wollah Doddah to the pupils was the nightmare of intelligent schoolboys. He was sarcastic, mean-minded, and enforced an uncompromising discipline. In effect, he was like a sort of real life cross between Mr Squeers from Dickens' Nicholas Nickleby, and Mr Quelch, the tormentor of Billy Bunter. Curzon in an early letter to his mother described Wolley-Dod's house as 'a grim monstrous barrack'. Three years later the purgatory was continuing. Just before the Browning scandal broke, he again wrote to his mother 'he pitches upon me on every possible occasion, and makes my life as much of a burden as he can. I am so loaded with his punishments during the last week that I haven't had a moment to myself'. There was therefore some 'history' between Hornby, Wolley-Dod and Curzon before the balloon went up.

Hornby realised that a direct accusation of homosexuality would lead inevitably to denials, a furious row, press stories and probably the law courts. He therefore contrived to remove Browning on something of a technicality. Each housemaster was allowed forty pupils plus, with permission, three non-resident boys. In the September of 1875 Browning had omitted to obtain the necessary permission so the three had to be included in the forty residents. This meant that Browning lost his allowance on three boys. Browning went to see Hornby to ask for money for the non-resident three, but Hornby refused. The anticipated pedantic argument ensued, but Hornby would not budge. Two days later Browning received a letter telling him that his mastership would terminate at the end of the term. Hornby was careful to follow this up by sending another letter saying he had no complaint against Browning's character, and that none would be made.

Browning was in an extremely awkward position. The Act of Parliament governing the administration of Public Schools meant that headmasters could dismiss staff for no reason, or for a false reason. An appeal to the Governing Body was Browning's only hope. If successful this would have meant the dismissal of Hornby. Browning did appeal and came very close to succeeding, but by the casting vote of the Provost of Eton, the appeal was rejected. Browning predictably made a huge and theatrical fuss amongst his supporters of whom significantly only three or four were fellow masters, and complained about being thrown out after fifteen years, and how his mother and sister would lose their home as well. It was to no avail and in December 1875 Browning left Eton.

Stephen would have been aware of the drama unfolding and surely hoped that Browning would survive. His father certainly did. Sir James wrote to Browning a long supportive letter. It concluded 'I have no reason whatever to believe that on any one occasion did you do anything which derogated in the least degree from your character as a schoolmaster, a gentleman or a man of honour. Nothing surprised me so much in the whole matter as the extremely trifling, I might almost say puerile, character of the charges which he made against you'. Another indignant supporter was the author and art critic, John Ruskin. He wrote in the December just as Browning was leaving 'As I heard with profound regret and a most bitter sense of the injustice done you that you were leaving Eton. What I have been permitted to see of the relations existing between your pupils and you seemed to me completely to realise the ideas of vital, affectionate and enduringly beneficent education'. The matter of Browning's 'irrepressible attentions' to Curzon were not entirely submerged, but it was treated as a secondary, if bitter, issue. Hornby forbade the two from meeting – a move that promoted the row into a spectator sport for all Etonians past and present. Doubtless many of them were keen enthusiasts of the sport of Kings and would have wagered on the outcome. The banning edict and the reasons for it reached Curzon's father, Lord Scarsdale, a pillar of probity. He wrote to Browning 'I exceedingly regret this very unpleasant complaint of Mr Wolley-Dod's with reference to your conduct towards my son George. I am fully aware of your warm feelings and give you full credit for acting from the purest motives'. Arthur Benson fumed 'it was a tyrannical and short sighted act'.

The fire and brimstone did not matter. Browning had gone and Hornby had prevailed. He had achieved his strategic objective by crafty tactics, which Browning was too complacent to anticipate or to thwart.

Chapter 3

A Man 'Flawed by Abysmal Fatuity'

Whatever the rights and wrongs of the matter, Hornby had shown much courage in dealing with a festering situation, and he had managed to remove one of Eton's most recalcitrant and embedded figures. Browning had been playing for high stakes. If he had followed Sir James Stephen's advice and taken the matter to court, the case could have led into questions about child molestation. If Browning won then Hornby would be sacked, but if he lost he risked a further case being brought against him. If he lost that case too he could have gone to prison for life. If all this had happened prior to 1861, Browning would have been hanged. He was lucky. The dispute remained within the walls of Eton, and Browning emerged with his character intact, although without a job. He was soon appointed by King's College, Cambridge as the head of history, and remained there until his retirement. He died in 1923.

Nor was Browning the only master Hornby was pleased to see the back of. He became concerned that another master had cultivated too close relations with certain boys but this time the work was done for him by outside forces. William Johnson, another Apostle and fine poet, had to resign his post in 1872 following a homosexual scandal with the Earl of Rosebery. His legacy to Eton was the composition of the Eton Boating Song. Hornby continued as headmaster until 1884 after which be became Provost of Eton until his death in 1909. In the eyes of the school and its Governing Body he was completely vindicated.

When Browning left Eton his boarding house was broken up. Some boys went to new houses and a few remained with Browning's successor. As was his custom in school holidays Browning organised short tours abroad with one or more selected pupils. He had been doing this regularly for years, and now he invited four boys who had also left Eton at the end of December to accompany him to Leipzig in early 1876. Stephen got wind of this trip and asked if he could come too. Browning readily agreed, after all he had been his counsellor since Thorpe Mandeville days. He later described Stephen as 'the most brilliant young man with whom I ever came into contact', including, presumably Curzon. The party stayed at Hotel Hauffe and their time was spent in academic study, visiting old battlefields, going to the opera and to the Gewandhaus concerts. Stephen only stayed for the Leipzig part of the tour, as he had to return for the new term. On his way home Stephen's suitcases were lost near Brussels, so he 'bribed a man heavily to get hold of my luggage somehow'. The bribe was 10/- (50p). Fortunately this worked, and the only casualty was one piece of china.

As has been mentioned earlier, Thorpe Mandeville School had been a happy hunting ground for Browning, and at least two other boys from that school, recruited by Browning, went with him on foreign holidays. In the summer of 1871 Browning took James Welldon to Italy. Welldon was sixteen at the time and not in good health. Three years later Browning again went abroad with Welldon this time to Norway. His last tour as an Eton master was also with Welldon, to Meyringen in the Alps in the summer of 1875. Welldon or 'Door' to his friends was appointed less than ten years later headmaster of Harrow, and amongst his charges was the young Winston Churchill. He ended up as Bishop of Calcutta. His religious views always put him at odds with his colleagues in the Cambridge Apostles, and he became remembered as the last of the Apostolic churchmen.

Another boy from Thorpe Mandeville was Martin Gosselin. Browning was not hesitant in describing his feelings about him. 'I made his acquaintance first when he was a pupil of my brother's at Thorpe Mandeville; he was then about twelve years old. He had a beautiful and striking face and a noble bearing. We were deeply attached to each other'. Browning took him on three tours abroad from Eton, the first in 1867, to Italy, Germany and Portugal. One particularly enjoyable outing was at Easter in 1875 with Gerald Balfour, brother of the future prime minister. Predictably enough Balfour gave Browning robust support in his fracas with Hornby later that year. By this time Balfour was at Trinity College, Cambridge and an Apostle. The two of them drove through the hazardous Abruzzi countryside in northern Italy, and visited many of the picturesque towns in the area. There were innumerable other overseas trips around Europe with the boys of his choice in the holiday periods, although there was no mention that George Curzon, his nemesis, was amongst them. In the circumstances of his dismissal from Eton, Browning may have chosen to edit out references to Curzon in his account of that period.

However, in the Christmas break of 1877 when Curzon was still at Eton, Lord Scarsdale gave his son permission to tour the French Riviera and parts of northern Italy with Browning. He had complete trust in Browning's integrity. There was nothing Hornby could do about it. The two were meeting in the holiday period and the trip had Lord Scarsdale's approval. During their visit to Milan a photograph of Browning and Curzon was taken, posed together with Browning's hand resting gently on his companion's shoulder. Curzon was 19, Browning 41. In Browning's lengthy autobiography this photograph is featured, along with four other illustrations – all of Browning. They went abroad again twice, and in 1902 when Curzon was Viceroy, Browning visited him in India. Browning and Curzon had by the late 1870s become friendly with Oscar Wilde, and in early 1880 he asked both of them for help. Wilde was struggling financially, and decided that he would like to be an inspector of schools. Accordingly he wrote to Browning asking for a recommendation. 'Will you do me a good service and write a testimonial of what you think my ability for a position in the Education Office or Schools Inspectorship would be? Any Education work would be very congenial to me. I think your name would carry a good deal of weight with it in a matter of this kind. The Duke of Richmond is the President of the Council in whose hands the appointments rest'. Wilde knew Browning had taught at Eton for many years but he was not aware of the circumstances five years earlier when Browning was forced to resign. Wilde also approached George Curzon asking him to use his influence with Edward Stanhope, who was involved in making the appointment. 'You could give me great help by writing a letter to say that I am a man of some brains. I don't know Stanhope personally and am afraid he may take the popular idea of me as a real idler'. Stanhope was a leading politician towards the end of the 19th century. Amongst the posts he held were Colonial Secretary, and Secretary for War. Curzon did what he could, but Browning's intervention was, unsurprisingly, not helpful, and Wilde failed in his mission.

The Cambridge Apostles was, and is, a debating society. It was originally known as the Cambridge Conversazione Society, which was founded in 1820. It was set up for undergraduates to discuss literary, political and religious matters, and it was called the Apostles as there were twelve founder members. It attracted some of the brightest minds in Cambridge, particularly from Trinity College, and election to the Society was seen as a considerable intellectual achievement. The Apostles did have a feeder club from which it often recruited new members. It was called the Chitchat Club and it was well established and respected. It was formed in 1860 with a membership based mainly on King's and Trinity Colleges. It met on Saturday evenings between 10.00 pm and midnight, and held literary and political discussions. The papers presented were not always of great intellectual merit and sometimes served as an excuse for a convivial get-together. Towards the end of the evening, claret, coffee, anchovies on toast (or 'whales'), were served, and snuff provided. These trappings were copied from the Apostles. It was both archaic and civilized. Possible recruits for the Apostles were 'interviewed' during an afternoon walk and probed for their philosophical leanings and for their social preferences. The Apostles had always had an undercurrent of homosexuality, and this became more pronounced towards the end of the 19th century. Partly because of this, the Society was secretive and self-protective. So, although membership was prestigious, it was also rather mysterious, and outsiders never quite knew who belonged. Oscar Browning was a member for sixty-five years, yet there is no mention of the Apostles' existence in his account of his life. This was not self-effacement, but because he believed it was not appropriate to discuss the Society's business. In fact he was a pivotal member throughout his membership. In the book The Cambridge Apostles 1820-1914 by WC Lubenow, Browning's name appears on fifty-eight pages. Only Apostolic icons John Maynard Keynes, Henry

Sidgwick, and Lytton Strachey receive more attention. This properly reflects Browning's significance to the Society, and why he was considered 'among the high priests of this sexual cult'.

Predictably several of the Apostles leaped to Browning's defence in his battle with John Hornby. Samuel Butcher, later MP for Cambridge, wrote to Hornby to appeal against the decision. Alfred Lyttelton, Henry Sidgwick, William Harcourt and Montagu Butler all weighed in with their outrage. James Welldon, one of Browning's holiday companions also protested to Hornby. Most of them were, or had been classicists, so there was an attempt to settle old scores in respect of Hornby's policy to widen the curriculum. Browning had by this time been an Apostle for seventeen years and most of the people who came to his aid shared his sexual preferences. They knew perfectly well Browning's proclivities, and saw the dismissal as a collective insult. They had no interest in his misdemeanours at Eton, and indeed they were provocatively supportive. Two years after Browning arrived at King's he was made President of the College's annual dinner.

Browning regarded the Apostles as 'one of the strongest intellectual forces in England or even in the world'. Yet for all his enthusiasm Browning had detractors who grew more vocal as time went on. His protégé at Thorpe Mandeville and Eton, James Welldon, criticised him for forcing his opinions 'down the throats of everyone who meets you'. Arthur Benson said that he was 'wallowing in that dreadful slough of self' and once having to listen to a Browning lecture, amused himself by counting the times he referred to 'I'. The total comfortably exceeded one thousand. Gradually he became regarded as little more than a self-important buffoon. His reputation reached its nadir when he took to inviting 'rough trade' to his rooms at

King's. This included soldiers, sailors and stable lads. Few nights passed without a 'horny handed companion, in case he was seized by sudden illness'. It has been suggested that the 'Hello Sailor' greeting was based on these activities, and that the naval term for homosexual 'Brown Hatter' is an abbreviation of a 'Browning Hatter'. A ribald legacy that would have shocked the vain Browning.

Hugh Macnaghten writing some fifty years after the event took place, had a more balanced view of the Hornby affair. He felt Browning had been responsible for his own downfall, that he talked and acted injudiciously. He thought Browning enjoyed the brazenness of situations that could be misinterpreted. Macnaghten actually witnessed one of these occasions. When six other boys came to one of Browning's tea parties, Macnaghten saw for himself how unscrupulous he was in his partisanship. Even WC Lubenow writing about the Apostles having described the support for Browning, admits that Browning was difficult to defend 'with his obnoxious behaviour, his rudeness, and his pomposity'. Later on Montague James, another King's Fellow came to dislike Browning intensely. He quoted Browning's comment 'I far prefer life among the undergraduates to life among the schoolboys: schoolboys always laugh at me, undergraduates don't'. James regarded this opinion as 'the most pathetic utterance of Oscar Browning that ever I heard'. Browning's remark stemmed from his endless bitterness towards Eton which continued for the rest of his days, and which became tiresome for his colleagues, many of whom sided with Hornby. Edward 'Fred' Benson, Arthur's brother, was even more damning. He delivered the terminal judgment, 'he was flawed by abysmal fatuity'.

Chapter 4

Floreat Etona

From his arrival at Eton, Stephen stood out from the other boys. He was unusually strongly built and gave the impression of strength. His features were clear cut and his eyes piercing. When he walked his hands hung stiffly by his sides rather like a Western film hero. It was at Eton that he acquired the nickname 'Jem', an old derivative of his name, which stayed with him for the rest of his life. As he grew older he was much admired by the younger boys who liked his vigorous nature and sharp intellect. He was so clear and persuasive in his views that they felt compelled to agree with him. Equally, he was happiest in their company. There is no doubt he had an influence over them sometimes in less than desirable ways. For example he wrote a very questionable poem to a younger contemporary referred to as ATM, which included the lines:

> 'Suck placid K: the world will be thy debtor
> Though thine eyes water, and thine heart grows faint,
> Suck and the less thou likest it the better:
> Suck for our sake and utter no complaint'.

The boy in question was Arthur Thomas Marson. He was two years younger than Stephen and after Eton, he went on to Trinity College.

The eccentricities, which would always be characteristic of Stephen were evident at Eton. He had a large room on the right hand side of Upper Passage. On the day when most of the school had gone to Lord's for the Harrow match, Stephen stayed behind to study in his room for the History prize. Hugh Macnaghten, a friend, was passing and seeing the door open went in to find Stephen wearing a surplice and sitting in a bath full of water. The weather was very hot and Stephen had donned the surplice in case a maid came in. He was not in the least put out. Shortly afterwards Stephen, who disapproved of gambling heard Macnaghten recounting a fine day out he had had at Ascot. He delivered a sharp kick from behind, and followed up with the message 'if you must make a damned fool of yourself, the less you say of it the better'.

Arthur Benson told the story of how Stephen had mimicked the Captain of the School to his face for which he was told to submit to a caning. Having taken advice from the Vice Provost, Francis Cornish, this he duly did. However, Stephen's popularity and the general dislike of the Captain meant that when the Captain appeared for supper in the Hall, all the boys got up and walked out in silence. It was an impressive display of support. One of Stephen's weaknesses was a tendency to lateness. In one of his poems 'Early School' written just after he left Eton, he ended with the line 'the glorious institution of always being late'. He would regularly turn up late for chapel, which, his agnosticism may have had something to do with, so much so that he was threatened with punishment. He would time his late entrance just when the headmaster, Hornby, was praying, and as Hornby opened his eyes, Stephen would be in his place. It was deliberate and theatrical. Once he even feigned a nosebleed to keep out of chapel until the sermon, which he wanted to hear, was due. On another occasion a colleague had been deputed to wake Stephen. This was done but Stephen returned to sleep, then woke in a panic. His lateness was only partly contrived. In a letter whilst at Eton to Oscar Browning he boasted 'I have only been late four times for Early School'.

His correspondence with Oscar Browning began soon after Stephen returned, on his own, from their visit to Leipzig. This was the occasion when his luggage went missing near Brussels on his way home. In February 1876 Stephen wrote 'I promised to write to inform you of my safe arrival as soon as I got here and proceed to do so after an interval of rather less than a month'. The letter to Browning was long and closely written, full of the minutiae of Eton life, and recorded a further threat of punishment if he was late back into his rooms again. It does seem that he was taking his work more seriously as he says 'I haven't done so much work as I ought or as I expected, but I'm really beginning to now'. He signed off 'Ever your affectionate pupil, JK Stephen'.

In another letter to Browning, this time in October of the same year, he again related events at Eton. Writing about 'Pop' he said 'they have elected a fearful set of people – many of them I should think you've scarcely heard of. By the way Curzon has got in of which I am exceedingly glad; why and how I don't know – he was strenuously blackballed last half'. Stephen's commitment to his studies continued 'I am going to work very hard this half, but have the misfortune to be the Keeper of the Wall which implies far more business than I should have thought'. The letter was written three weeks before his legendary performance in the Wall Game. The tone of the letter was earnest and respectful. Stephen finished up 'I hope your rooms and so on at King's (Cambridge) are satisfactory. I wish I was going to hear your history lesson. Believe me. Yours affectionately JK Stephen.

Even though Browning had left Eton for more than a year, Stephen still addressed him in a letter dated January 1877 as

'My dear Tutor'. It took a further two years, well after the time that Stephen had left Eton before he felt able to write 'Dear OB'. Stephen's father encouraged their relationship. In the January letter Stephen thanked Browning for an invitation to Cambridge, made through Sir James, and looked forward to spending three or four days there. Sir James seemed to have a view of Browning that is difficult to understand. He allowed his son to go abroad with Browning, to stay in his rooms at Cambridge and generally encouraged him to foster a friendship. Either Stephen's father was extremely naïve, or he was indifferent to the likely influences. Perhaps he regarded this sort of friendship as a public school rite of passage. This exchange of letters, visits and pleasantries was to last for the rest of Stephen's life.

Stephen was a prolific letter writer. As well as to Browning, he corresponded with friends, acquaintances, club members and family. One letter in the latter category written a couple of months before he left Eton was to his uncle Leslie (Stephen). For some reason he spent nearly the whole letter singing the praises of a master called Cornish. Cornish was the deputy to Browning in Stephen's house, and he became the school's Vice Provost. His full name was Francis Warre Cornish and Stephen says of him 'I don't think there is a better tutor than Cornish in any way. He is quite the best tutor'. For his part Cornish liked Stephen and noted the charm with which he addressed the staff and older boys. His view was that 'although he (Stephen) was careless on some matters upon which schoolmasters set a high value (probably punctuality), he always showed power and originality'.

Cornish was the closest friend Browning ever had. The two had been boys together at Eton where Browning admits 'Cornish had been an intimate friend of mine'. They progressed together to King's, Cambridge, and Browning describes them as 'Inseparable. We read together, played music together, made friends together'. To Browning, Cornish was 'like a pure and faultless spirit plunging into a cool, refreshing pool'. They spent holidays abroad together: a walking tour to northern Italy, Dresden in 1860, and the next year to Florence and Bonn, where they attended the Beethoven festival. Nearly fifty years later Browning dedicated his autobiography to Cornish with a poem.

To
F W Cornish
Vice-Provost Of Eton College

In youth we roamed, a merry land,
Through mead and desert, hand in hand,
With Dick and Henry, Charles and George,
The fetters of our life to forge,
We strove and quarrelled, fought and kissed,
And not a fount of joy was missed.
But George and Charles are grey and old,
And Jermyn's loving heart is cold;
And Henry's name is on his tomb,
And Dick has met the common doom;
And we, whose friendship stood the strain
Of driving storm and surging main,
Whate'er we seem in other's eyes
Are young, at least, in memories.
The last, the dearest of the crew,
I dedicate this book to you.

Oscar Browning
January 9, 1910

Despite Stephen's eccentricities, he was seen as one of an outstanding generation of boys, alongside such names as

George Curzon, Cecil Spring-Rice, RH Macaulay, Henry Goodhart and Oliver Vassall. Their interest lay in books, politics and ideas, which they pursued without any sign of a wish to be seen as intellectually superior. Vassall in particular, must have welcomed this academic escape for more mundane reasons. He was given a hard time by senior boys and masters. When they realised he had a mortal fear of milk, any punishment meted out to him involved drinking milk. This unpleasantness was led by a boy called George Lawrence, another protégé of Browning who was much taken by his angelic appearance. Browning took him on holiday to Switzerland. Vassall survived to become Father Vassall-Philips, the Redemptionist.

Arthur Benson was effusive in his praise of Stephen. He believed he had 'an extraordinary lucidity of view', 'an abundant sense of humour' and 'a marked sanity of judgement'. Benson was three years younger than Stephen, the right age for him to be one of Stephen's acolytes and admirers. Today Benson is remembered as the author of the Empire hymn 'Land of Hope and Glory'. It was certainly a prevalent view that Stephen's opinions were direct, fearless, and sharply thought through. He came to Eton as a classicist, but never reached the top grade. The prizes he secured related to history, literature and the law. With his father's agreement he gave up classics when he left Eton and took up history and law at Cambridge.

At Eton, Stephen had other interests, which like rowing, amounted to little more than hobbies. He enjoyed them, but did not take them seriously. One of these was music, although he knew nothing of its formal composition. Another was singing. This came to the fore after the College Supper, a celebration to mark the end of the autumn term. Beer was freely available and behaviour soon degenerated. At this point Stephen would begin to sing, loudly and with much solemnity. He stood before his audience, parodying the great tenors. As the performance reached its climax, he would take on an air of gravity and fury, then bow and allow a few moments of dramatic silence before the Hall rocked with laughter and applause.

Stephen's capacity to enjoy himself was matched by his ability to work hard, and to win prizes that were important and prestigious. His first success was the English Essay Prize in 1875, he was then only 16. He followed this by winning the History Prize in both the following years. Also in 1877 he was one of the 'select' for the Newcastle Prize. This was an award for the best paper on classics and divinity subjects. Stephen's success meant he received £50 for each of his years at Cambridge. Finally in 1878 he won the Declamation, a prize given for public speaking. Yet all these awards were dwarfed by his best achievement – a scholarship to King's College, Cambridge.

Unlike his father, Stephen thoroughly enjoyed his time at Eton. From the outset he was big enough to look after himself so bullying, which had so blighted his father, was not a problem. As he progressed through the school his various talents, whether academic, sporting, or social, became increasingly recognised. Also unlike his father, there was never a question of leaving the school to study elsewhere. In fact Stephen did leave the school one term early. He convinced his father that once his scholarship to Cambridge had been secured his time would be better spent going abroad rather than serving out the last few weeks. This meant Sir James had to write to John Hornby for formal agreement. This was a rather awkward task, as Sir James had taken a virulently opposite view to Hornby in the Browning affair, and although two years had passed, old differences would not have been forgotten. Sir James duly wrote a civil letter explaining the situation and Hornby replied equally politely, even warmly. His letter was dated 18 February 1878.

'My dear James Stephen,

Thank you for your kind letter. Your son has done <u>very</u> well at Eton, but I am not surprised that you have determined to take him away now. He is old in mind and will probably gain more by going abroad after he is done with the Newcastle and King's examinations than by staying for another Summer Half at Eton'.

Hornby did gently allude to some old issues. He repeated his belief that more modern subjects had had to be added to the traditional classics in the curriculum. However he put out an olive branch with the phrase 'I hope the classical element will be predominant'. He ends with a hint of self justification in his view of the future 'I think we can give a good account of prospects compared with thirty years ago and I hope things may be easier for my successor for what has been done in my time. Ever sincerely, JJ Hornby'. A truce of sorts had been declared.

During the summer of 1878 Stephen visited France, and whilst in Paris met up with Browning. The two were attending a ceremony in the Champs Elysees when they became separated by the crowd, and although Stephen looked around for 'the white hats' he failed to find Browning. In a letter to Browning, in French, written from the Rue Clotaire, he apologised for the mix-up and for not saying goodbye the following morning, 'but I didn't get up. I am not very practical, especially when I go to bed at 2 o'clock'. He then moved on to Hotel Joseph to visit someone called 'P' who failed to get out of bed during Stephen's half hour visit. The matter of accommodation at Cambridge was clearly on his mind and he expressed hopes of getting into the Fellows Building, and that he would be happy to take temporary rooms up to Christmas if he could then stay at Fellows. He finished the letter to Browning by thanking him for his gifts 'which I shall always treasure'. It was a friendly, gossipy letter with no apparent undercurrent or innuendo.

Stephen's last two years at Eton had been the most productive in the way of prizes, performances in the Wall Games, and contributions to the cultural and debating ethos of Eton. In no way was he in his father's shadow. The reverse was more true, and in terms of overall success Stephen's reputation contrasted with that of his diffident parent. Perhaps Stephen enjoyed Eton too much and later he spent too much time looking back at these halcyon days. For a long time he would bring a 'Wall' team down to play the Collegers, and it was recalled how during these visits how he would lounge about, talking endlessly with the boys, perhaps like Caesar visiting his favourite imperial post, although a few of the more perceptive boys wondered what he did for a living. Extracts from a poem, 'My Old School', written by Stephen some years later encapsulate his enduring love of Eton:

> 'There's a street that's alive with boys and masters,
> And ah! There's a feeling of home for me
> For my boyhood's triumphs, delights, disasters
> Successes and failures were here, you see'

> 'And if sometimes I've laughed in my rhymes at Eton
> Whose glory I could never jeopardise

Yet I'd never a joy that I could not sweeten,
Or a sorrow I could not exorcise'

'By the thought of my school, and the brood that's bred there
Her bright boy faces and keen young life;
And the manly stress of the hours that sped there,
And the stirring pulse of her daily strife'

'And it is not a form of words, believe me
To say I am yours while my pulses beat,
And whatever garlands the fates may weave me
I'll lay right gladly at Eton's feet'

True, he did write a poem just after he left Cambridge, called the 'Ode on a retrospect of Eton College'. It opened with the lines:

'Ye bigot spires, ye Tory towers
That crown the watery lea,
Where grateful science still adores
The aristocracy'

It ends with the words 'That here, where ignorance is bliss, Tis folly to be wise'. The poem was a parody of the work of Thomas Gray who published, over a century earlier, 'Ode on a Distant Prospect of Eton College'. Much of Stephen's poetry were parodies or adaptations of earlier works by major poets. He applied this treatment to Robert Browning, Wordsworth, and even Shakespeare. It was a legitimate and popular form of light verse. Stephen's parody of Gray was always intended as satire and did not reflect his real affection and respect for the college. He was a dedicated Etonian through and through. Floreat Etona should have been engraved on his tomb.

Chapter 5

On the Banks of the Cam

No sooner had Stephen entered King's College, Cambridge in the autumn of 1878, than he found Oscar Browning waiting for him. When Browning had been dismissed from Eton he wondered if he should start his own preparatory school, which would provide a home for his mother and sister as well as a good income. However, he rejected this as he 'knew very little of boys under the age of thirteen'. For a brief while he thought he should go to the Bar. It now seems inevitable that he would return to King's, the college of his undergraduate days. Browning had gone up to King's from Eton in July 1856, and he had always enjoyed his visits to Cambridge. In addition a new history school had just been set up, and the College was keen to employ him. So a round peg was fitted into a round hole.

Stephen got his accommodation wish and found rooms on the ground floor of the Fellows building known as Gibbs. They were large, rather dark, and the front room was panelled and painted dark green. The inner sitting room contained a big work desk and a wooden writing chair. It was here that Stephen spent most of his working day. The rest of the furniture was a collection of miscellaneous pieces. Nothing matched, and Stephen was certainly not interested in a co-ordinated effect when it came to furnishing his rooms. When he left Cambridge Arthur Benson, who had just arrived, took over the rooms and bought most of Stephen's furniture. According to Brian

Masters in his book 'The Life of E F Benson', when Arthur Benson died in 1925, Stephen's wooden chair was bequeathed to Magdalene College. Benson had been the Master at Magdalene. However the College now has no knowledge of the chair, so it must have fallen by the wayside long ago. Browning, who lived in Wilkins's Buildings, had more elegant tastes. He liked Turkish carpets, floral wallpapers and 'bits of statuary picked up for a song in Italy, fine engravings and dainty bronzes'. He also collected furniture on his travels in Europe and India. When he was in Oporto, an old colleague at Eton William Johnson, found him two valuable leather chairs and a rosewood and silver cabinet made in Goa, which he promptly had shipped back to Cambridge. The rooms themselves were quite small, but he grew to like them, and kept them until he retired.

Clubs and societies had always had an appeal for Stephen and he soon set about joining those that interested him. It was only a matter of days before Browning had inveigled him into the Political Society. This was a society that Browning had founded in October 1876 and its purpose was to allow undergraduates the opportunity to debate political issues. Herbert, Stephen's elder brother, was a founder member. The club's conditions were simple and did not change throughout Browning's presidency, which lasted until 1908. The main four rules were:

- The number of members should be limited to twelve
- That members be elected below the rank of MA
- That no member be elected except unanimously
- That no member be expected to write more than one essay in each term

Stephen was voted in as a member on 14 October 1878 and six weeks later read a paper to show 'International Law does not exist, and probably never would'. A little later he submitted a sharply argued thesis entitled 'The Object of Government'. Stephen was by no means in the thrall of Browning. At one point he had the temerity to chastise the President by writing in the minutes of 25 October that 'the President violated the fundamental rules of the Society, speaking out of his turn. He wishes the secretary to put upon record his apology for this breach of duty and to explain that it is not, nor it cannot be, a precedent'. It was a nerveless rebuff to the Society's founder, and creator of the rules. Stephen continued his membership after he left Cambridge. On one occasion in 1884 to the motion 'Were there party distinctions before the Flood?' he managed to vote 'yes' and 'no'. Browning also had a hand in creating the Eighty Club, so named because that was the year of its inception. It was intended as a discussion group for 'young men of character'. The dinners were small, sociable and occasionally very distinguished, such as the time when both Gladstone and Asquith attended. It was right up Stephen's street and he needed little persuasion to join. It was at an Eighty Club meeting that Stephen made one of his rare protestations of political allegiance when he rather angrily affirmed that he was 'still a Tory'.

Another club of which Stephen soon became a member was the Cambridge Apostles. His father had been elected a member in 1847, when he was only eighteen. Sir James remained an active member for nearly forty years, which partly accounts for his faith in Oscar Browning. Stephen became an Apostle in 1879. In 1881 Sir James came to a meeting of the Society and Stephen presented a paper. However, he does not seem to have been a very enthusiastic member, and the obligation to attend all meetings proved too much of a discipline. Stephen resigned in 1882, and became an 'Angel'. This meant he was free to come to meetings as and when he liked. He did occasionally attend as on 2 May 1885 when he opposed the proposal 'Do we believe in God?' This may have been the occasion of his father's last meeting with the Apostles. He had become tired of their rituals and jokes, and sometime in 1885 he gave a farewell dinner.

From his time at Eton and throughout his Cambridge days, Stephen was an avowed agnostic. His views may have been formed as a child when he became aware of his father's indifference to religious matters, and, to him, the odium of his mother's excessive beliefs. A few years earlier he had met Nathaniel Wedd, a fellow Apostle, and both of them filled a religious void with a love of poetry, in Wedd's case Shelley's.

The Apostles were not entirely unhappy to accept Stephen's resignation. Some members had become aware of his over aggressive style, and use of bad language. It was a habit that manifested itself at Eton. There, his fellow pupils realised Stephen was capable of sudden outbursts of explosive language. It did not happen very often, but when it did, it was direct, abusive and highly scornful. The boys feared these eruptions. This may have been an indication of the problems to come. Even though Stephen's time as an Apostle was short he was remembered. Nearly sixty years later in December 1950 GM Trevelyan proposed a toast at the Founder's Feast at King's College. He paid tribute to the 'great Apostles who had been members of King's'. He included Stephen 'of unfulfilled renown'. The Feast takes place every year on 6 December which is the date of St Nicholas, the patron saint of Henry VI who founded both Eton and King's College. Trevelyan had a brilliant academic career based on Trinity College as a lecturer and professor of history. He was later the Master, and was an active member in Leslie Stephen's 'Sunday Tramps'. Stephen also belonged to another society that was an off-shoot of the Apostles and was the brain-child of Henry Sidgwick. It was called the Ad Eundem Club and was made up of twenty members divided equally between Cambridge and Oxford, resident and non-resident. Its purpose was to encourage university reform and met once a term to discuss university affairs over dinner. Nearly all the Cambridge members were Apostles. Stephen once missed a meeting and wondered if this would put his membership in jeopardy. However the rules stated that members only had to attend two meetings in any two year period. Stephen remained a member until his death.

The other important club, which Stephen joined soon after leaving Eton was the Savile Club. Although it had nothing to do with Cambridge, several of its members were Apostles. It was set up in London in 1868 by the leading literati of the period including Oscar Browning. Over the years membership has included Robert Louis Stevenson, HG Wells, Rudyard Kipling, William Walton and Edward Elgar. Wells described the Savile as 'The Athenaeum for the living'. It was and remains a gentlemen's club. Membership for women, requiring a two thirds voting majority, moves closer each year, and now may be expected within the next decade. The club has always valued friendliness and informality, and this combination of talent and sociability appealed to Stephen. He was proposed in 1880 by his brother Herbert, who had joined the previous year, and seconded by Sir Sidney Colvin, the poet and professor of Fine Art at Cambridge. Four of his supporters were Apostles, including Bernard Holland and Francis Balfour. Balfour was killed climbing on Mont Blanc with the Alpine Club two years later. The Savile Club was in Piccadilly at the time, walking distance from Stephen's home in De Vere Gardens. By all accounts Stephen was a regular and enthusiastic member. He proposed several men for membership who ended up in the Directory of National Biography or Who's Who. In October 1888, the Rev. WJ Loftie put forward Oscar Wilde for membership, and Stephen was one of the supporters who counter signed Wilde's application. It was probably through Oscar Browning that Stephen first met Wilde at Cambridge. In November 1879 Wilde wrote to Browning accepting an invitation to visit him for 'the festivities'. This was a reference to the Founders Feast. Wilde did attend the celebrations, and since all the members of King's College would have been present, and bearing in mind Browning's friendship with Stephen, an introduction would almost certainly have taken place. On two or three subsequent occasions Wilde stayed with Browning at King's during Stephen's time at Cambridge. This was the background for Stephen's support for Wilde several years later. Although thirty-one members backed Wilde's candidature, the application did not go through. The committee did not have to state its reasons for rejection, and they were never known. Wilde was by this time a controversial personality and it would not be surprising if one of the committee had opposed him. The Savile Club does not operate a blackball system as such, but when there is an objection, the application is simply postponed indefinitely. Loftie's own career unravelled when he was involved in the seduction of a parlour maid. He had been assistant chaplain at the Chapel Royal in the Savoy Hotel, and an expert in gravel, (he would spend his spare time examining the substrata of old buildings), but he felt the scandal would damage beyond repair his image of a serious, cerebral churchman.

One possible reason for Wilde's non-acceptance may have been an erratic relationship with two of his sponsors, WE

Henley and Henry James. Henley was a fine poet and journalist (and a member of the Ad Eundem Club with Stephen), but he was quarrelsome and it is quite likely that Henley withheld his support when it came to a vote. Wilde also had a volatile relationship with Henry James. James said of him 'Wilde is a fatuous fool, tenth rate cad' and Wilde responded that James 'wrote English prose as if it were a painful duty'. In view of this animosity it is surprising James ever signed Stephen's form. Under a cover of secrecy either Henley or James or both, could have ensured Wilde's application fell into abeyance. Wilde may not have been much concerned at the outcome. When Henley first suggested membership Wilde replied 'As for proposing me for the Savile that is of course one of your merry jests'. The club's membership took no exception to Wilde's characteristic remark 'Ah! The Savile Club, a true republic of letters; not a sovereign among 'em'.

The nature of the club and its proximity to his home meant that Stephen was often there, and he was proposing new members up to the end of the 1880s. Stephen was keen to set up his own club, and this he did in 1879 when he formed the Twice a Fortnight, or TAF Club. The club's minute book marks against Stephen's name 'Fundator'. Membership was drawn from King's and Trinity Colleges, and from former pupils of leading public schools such as Eton and Harrow. It was not a serious political or literary group, but it served to provide entertainment on Sunday evenings instead of going into Hall for supper which, Montague James described as 'intolerable'. After a cold meal, members could talk, play the piano, sing or indeed amuse each other in any way they wished. The club exuded a friendly, easy-going atmosphere, exactly in accordance with the founder's wishes. Although its nature was hedonistic it did attract some members who later had distinguished careers, such as Walter Headlam, Gerald Duckworth, and Edward Benson. Benson, son of the Archbishop of Canterbury, became a recognised intellectual, and author of over 100 books. He also had the 'distinction' of being the lover of Oscar Wilde and Lord Alfred Douglas. The Ford brothers, Henry and Walter attended regularly. Henry was the artist, often caricatures, and Walter the singer. Neither took themselves too seriously, and enjoyed the casual lifestyle that TAF offered. The club stopped meeting when Stephen left Cambridge, but four years later in 1886 Montague James and some colleagues resurrected it. Its formula was much as before with dinners, music, and conversation the central features. At this stage James was its leader, but he grew tired of the group's exclusiveness and what one member described as the 'Love-feast of the Clan', and he quietly resigned. James was an authority on scripts from the Middle Ages and a renown writer of ghost stories. He had a formidable intellect, and it was said he could complete the Times crossword at breakfast time before his egg was soft boiled.

For a few years there was an annual dinner at Cambridge and members were entitled to bring a guest. For these dinners there would be a main event, and once there was a re-enactment of a University scandal. It concerned two senior dons Dr Westcott and J E (Johnny) Nixon. The former knifed to death a woman who sold apples, but the murder weapon turned up in the possession of Nixon. Nixon was arrested whilst giving a lecture on Rhetoric. In due course he was tried, found guilty and hanged. Westcott observed the proceedings with an act of great concern for his friend, but made no move to intervene. Nixon had been one of the University's great eccentrics. Handicapped by having only one eye and an artificial right hand, he was uncontrollably hyperactive and argumentative. He wore a black tailcoat for tennis and rode around Cambridge on a tricycle. Every week he conducted 'impromptu singing sessions which culminated in Tintara wine, hot teacakes, and Borneo cigars'. The TAF club finally came to an end with Stephen's death in 1892.

Chapter 6

A Friend called Harry

One very sad event, which happened in July 1880, about half way through Stephen's undergraduate days was the death of his sister Frances from rheumatic fever. She was fifteen. Stephen sent a long letter dated 2 August to another sister Katherine describing the funeral. He wrote 'Herbert got the wreath – it was stephanotis I think – and there were two others from Lady Lawrence and from Aunt Emmy. The coffin was made of brown wood and covered with purple cloths, and the hearse was quite open. I think everything was pretty as it could be'. Stephen then set off into a lengthy philosophical consideration about the meaning of life and death and how to cope with it. He was clearly upset at having to bury a younger sister. He finished the letter with:

> 'Goodbye dearest Kate. I hope you and Helen and the little ones are all feeling happier. Please give my love to them and to Mother when she comes. Ever your loving brother JKS'.

Katherine herself had an exemplary academic career and became Principal of Newnham College, Cambridge. She was the oldest of Sir James's children. She survived her father's anti-feminism and found herself work at Newnham. She was appointed the college's librarian, then vice principal and finally Principal for nine years from 1911. She was most conscientious in her family responsibilities. She wrote to her mother every day, cared for her cousin Laura when her mental disorders became serious, and never ceased to try to help her brother James right up to his death. She was a particularly sensible and hardworking woman.

At Cambridge Stephen met up with a man called Harry Wilson. He had been educated at Rugby School, and went to Trinity College as a Foundation Scholar at the same time as Stephen entered King's. He was a classicist, and won prizes for his poetry, which he wrote mainly as a hobby. He was the son of a Norfolk vicar, and family money was limited so he had to rely on his own talent and ambition. In this he succeeded wonderfully well. He became a barrister in the Colonial Office's legal department, and won a worldwide reputation as a leading colonial administrator. He was knighted by George V, and held empire related business positions such as chairman of British Overseas Stores, and chairman of the North Charterland Exploration Company. However all these accomplishments were a long way from his days at Trinity, and his friends there would not have recognised the establishment figure he became.

Stephen first came into contact with Wilson almost as soon as they came up to Cambridge in the autumn of 1878. Wilson had become infatuated with Stephen's younger brother Henry, who was also very good looking. Fortunately Wilson and Stephen were kindred spirits, enjoyed each other's company and became close friends. Wilson did not hide his feelings for Henry. He kept a detailed diary, and against an entry about Henry, he noted 'I love him, I love him'. The diary and the references to Henry ran from November 1878 up to the time nine years later when he finally left Cambridge. Wilson and Henry frequently had breakfast and lunch together and as a Christmas gift Henry gave Wilson a volume of Keats poems.

Henry had introduced Wilson to his father early in the relationship, and in November of the following year Henry's mother, Lady Stephen and Henry Maine, a trusted family friend, came to lunch. Even at this stage Wilson was a social climber. Suddenly from a modest background he was mixing with a High Court judge and knight of the realm. No wonder he cultivated the Stephen family. It was a strategy he employed for the rest of his life.

The first mention in the diary of Stephen was in the evening of the same day that Wilson had lunched with Stephen's mother and Henry Maine. Thereafter the initials of both brothers cropped up regularly, sometimes on the same day. It seems Wilson's friendship with Stephen was not just a necessary by product of a route to Henry. He noted details about him in the diary, such as when he found him 'rushing about carving lunch'. Wilson told of walks with Stephen and Oscar Browning, who soon picked him out. One entry said 'take Maxwell to o.b's. He described Maxwell as 'blasé but talkative', so he should have gone down well with Browning. This was George Maxwell, by now up at Trinity from Eton. He was a Scot, and after he left Cambridge he took up an army career with the Scottish Borderers. Stephen's tendency for unpunctuality was still with him. He turned up late for a lunch with Wilson and some other guests including an Arthur Myers. Wilson described Myers as 'unbearable'.

Wilson led a very social life. The diary is dotted with accounts of lunches, suppers and parties. One of these ended with Stephen ('a judge's son!!!') giving a riotous rendition of 'Rule Britannia'. At another, with both the Stephen brothers present, it was poetry reading. The first week in December 1881 was an exciting one for Wilson. On the Saturday he went with Henry to Childerley and played a game of hide and seek. Later the same day came the dramatic entry, made in capital letters 'I am elected an Apostle'. The next day he recorded, again in joyous capital letters, 'I am very happy'. It was also the moment when he made his declaration of love for Henry. It sounded as if they were the best few days of his life. The day after he went with Henry to Granchester, just outside Cambridge, and the two took a trip up the river. However this idyll with Henry was coming to an end. On the 20 December 1881 Wilson notes in capital 'HLS goes down for good'. A few days earlier there had been a farewell dinner for Henry which Stephen, of course attended. At it, Wilson signed the Apostolic roll. A last game of tennis with Stephen, Henry and Henry Broadshaw, another of Oscar Browning's friends from Eton, who Wilson describes as 'pathetic', and then it was time to take Henry to the station. That night Wilson entered the sad words 'I feel how lonely shall I be'. This was by no means the end of the friendship. In April the next year the two undertook an extensive European tour to Paris, Italy and Switzerland. In Paris they visited Notre Dame, the Pantheon, went to the theatre to see 'Serge-Panine', and dined at L'Avocat des Dawes, then on to Versailles. Later back in Paris they took in the Louvre, and the Jardins de Luxembourg. Clearly Wilson was loving every minute. They then went on to Italy and Milan, Sirmio and Venice, followed by Switzerland and Basle, Avona and Waggis. It was the classical tour and could have been planned by Oscar Browning. By now Wilson's undergraduate four years at Cambridge were nearly over, and having been awarded First Class in Classical Tripos, he left in July 1882. He soon returned to Cambridge to work on various post graduate courses and in November went to see Stephen's celebrated performance as the hero Ajax in Sophicles's play at the Cambridge Theatre.

It was one of only two real attempts that Stephen made at

acting. His dominating personality and physical presence made him well suited to take the lead role. A critic noted 'his massive frame and generally noble appearance fitted him admirably'. Sometime later Montague James described the production as 'a great event, but a sad presage that he (Stephen) should have had to present that particular part'. In the play Ajax eventually went mad and committed suicide.

Sir James watched the play and had some reservations about his son 'exhibiting himself personally', but was mollified as he felt Stephen acted 'more like a gentleman amusing himself than like a professional performer'. Reports suggested this was true. His performance was viewed as passionate but without any real dramatic talent; his speech was considered hurried and his gestures stiff. It was another of Stephen's pleasures, not to be taken seriously but thoroughly enjoyed, and an opportunity for some energetic fun, especially at rehearsals. He was a member of the Amateur Dramatic Society, known as 'Footlights', which Oscar Browning had set up. A picture of the main characters in the cast, with Ajax at the centre, appeared in 'The Illustrated Sporting and Dramatic News' on 16 December 1882. Stephen looked suitably confident. Oscar Browning was in the audience. Ajax was the first of a long series of Greek plays that the University produced. Stephen was the star and his friend Harry Cust also had an important role. He was Teucer. The following year The Birds by Aristophanes was produced with Montague James in the lead role.

Stephen's other appearance as an actor was in the summer of 1883 at a large private house in London owned by a Lady Freke. Lillie Langtry had appeared on the same stage. An American lady Maud du Puy had been visiting friends in Cambridge, and they decided to take her to see the Greek rendition of The Tale of Troy. In a letter from Maud du Puy to her daughter Gwen, she said of

Stephen's performance 'Mr Stephen was Hector and acted remarkably well'. She added 'Lionel Tennyson as Ulysses would have been better had he known the part'. Lionel was the son of Alfred. In the audience that day were prime minister William Gladstone and the artist, Sir Frederic Leighton, who was in charge of the costumes and scenery.

At Cambridge and earlier at Eton, Stephen's occasional outbursts of bad language and temper had been noted. A trivial incident could upset him such as an occasion in July 1882. Stephen was travelling by train through the Belgian town of Malines when a fellow passenger accidentally trod on his foot and woke him up. This set his pen working with a fury:

'4th July, 1882, Malines, Midnight.

> Belgian, with cumbrous tread and iron boots,
> Who in the murky middle of the night,
> Designing to renew the foul pursuits
> In which thy life is passed, ill-favoured wight,
> And wishing on the platform to alight
> Where thou couldst mingle with thy fellow brutes,
> Didst walk the carriage floor (a leprous sight),
> As o'er the sky some baleful meteor shoots:
> Upon my slippered foot thou didst descend,
> Didst rouse me from my slumbers mad with pain,
> And laughedst loud for several minutes' space.
> Oh may'st thou suffer tortures without end:
> May fiends with glowing pincers rend thy brain,
> And beetles batten on thy blackened face!'

Even then there was something strange about the violence of his sadistic language.

In contrast to his time at Eton, Stephen did little at Cambridge that could be called athletic or sporting, although he was a member of the Rifle Club, and he did play some tennis in a foursome which usually included his brother and Harry Wilson. He became quite keen on the game and made reference to tennis in a poem:

'To see good Tennis! What diviner joy
Can fill our leisure, or our minds employ?'

Another club, which could loosely be described as athletic was the Sunday Tramps. It was founded by Stephen's uncle Leslie, and Stephen was persuaded to join in 1879. The club met on alternate Sundays during the summer months, and its members combined a substantial walk, perhaps twenty miles with some intellectual conversation. It was felt vigorous walking stimulated the mind. There were sixty members, but usually the turn out was about ten. There was no obligation for members ever to take part in a walk, and some never did. Although Stephen was certainly a member, there are no reports that he was actually tempted into a walk. His brothers Henry and Herbert also appeared on the roll call. One member, Arthur Butler, even composed a ballad to the Tramps. He was secretary of the Alpine Club, and had the classic credentials of Eton, Trinity and the Apostles to whom he was known as 'Pig'. The first verse of the work ran:

'If weary you grow at your books
Or dyspeptical after you've dined,
If your wife makes remarks on your looks,
If in short you feel somewhat inclined
For fresh air and a six hours' grind
And good metaphysical talk –
With a party of writers in Mind
You should go for a Sabbath day's walk.'

The society lasted fifteen years, and it took its last step in March 1895 after 252 outings.

Stephen was far more active in the area of debate and in particular the Cambridge Union. In his last year he was elected President, an honour going only to the best speakers. When the electoral contest reached its final stages Stephen put forward his case in an eleven verse poem. It was a masterpiece of self-promotion and little modesty. It began with these lines:

> 'I venture to suggest that I
> Am rather noticeably fit
> To hold the seat illumined by
> The names of Palmerston and Pitt'

And it concluded with:

> 'And since those early days, the same
> Success was crowned the self-same plan
> Profundity I cannot claim
> Respectability I can'

Once he spoke for an hour in defence of the Established Church. This at least showed his flexibility to take any side of a case, and to argue it persuasively, for in reality he was an agnostic. He was seen as a speaker 'with a natural bent towards dainty and exquisite language'. Nor did Stephen avoid the controversial. His views on the Home Rule for the Ireland issue were expressed in four lines of poetry which he put to the Cambridge Union in 1882:

> 'Respecting Ireland, I opine,
> That Ministers are in a mess.
> That Landlords rule by Right Divine,
> That Firmness will remove Distress'

It was Stephen's view that the Irish struggle for self-rule was an insult to the monarchy and the Tory party, and therefore to himself. It was embarrassing for Stephen that one of the most ruthless republican leaders at the time, was called James Stephens. Stephen was also a member, although less active, of the Philosophical Society and presented a long discourse without notes. This especially impressed Browning.

Stephen's undergraduate years were mostly spent in societies, writing poetry, and generally enjoying the fripperies of university life. Although it is true he was less responsive to formal tuition, he did have considerable conventional academic ability, and he won prizes to prove it. In 1880 he won the Member's Prize for an English essay. His subject was Lord Bolingbroke, an Etonian, statesman and man of letters who lived in the previous century. The following year Stephen took the inaugural Whewell Scholarship for international law. His father was proud of him and said in letters to friends 'he is a splendid young fellow. He will surpass me in good time and will be the fourth distinguished man of his name. He is a sturdier fellow than I was and writes better than I could at his age'. Also in 1881, Stephen won the Winchester Reading prize. This was awarded for reading out loud. His best achievement was to be awarded a First Class in the History Tripos in 1882, which secured his BA. This success was due in large part to the brilliance of his English essay. The prize was of particular merit as no one had reached the First Class level for two years. His second class degree in the Law Tripos was a slight disappointment, particularly to his father, who longed for him to have a legal career. It reflected the difficulty Stephen sometimes had 'to subdue his mind to the slavery of mechanical learning'. Nevertheless this setback did not hamper his legal ambitions, and when he left Cambridge in the summer of 1882, it was with the intention of being called to the Bar. So he moved back to London.

Chapter 7

A Royal Tutor

Stephen's objective on leaving Cambridge was to become a barrister, but it soon became evident that he was not fully committed to this life. He often returned to King's to attend social gatherings and he maintained his reputation for having the sharpest of minds. On one occasion he was listening to a dull, elderly clergyman deliver a sermon about the prospects of the immortal spirit. Stephen was alerted by the man using the line from Wordsworth, 'Heaven lies about us in our infancy', and Stephen was heard to mutter: 'That's no reason why you should lie about Heaven in your old age'. His talent for debating and conversation was undimmed, but to build a career he needed something more.

Soon after Stephen returned to London, he decided to spend some time in France and Germany, ostensibly to prepare for the Law Tripos. In reality it was more of a holiday. Whilst in Germany he visited Berlin and wrote to Browning from the Motz Strasse. It seemed no excursion was complete without some correspondence with his old tutor. It was during this tour that his travels took in Belgium and Malines where he wrote his indignant poem. It was the occasion when a man trod on his foot and woke him up on a train journey. It is likely that at some stage he met up with Oscar Browning who was in Malines at about the same time.

His concentration on his studies was further compromised

when he met the Prince and Princess of Wales in the summer of 1883. The meeting was arranged by the Rev. John Dalton, who had been in charge of the royal couple's sons, Edward and George during a three year cruise on HMS Bacchante between 1879 – 1882. Dalton had been told by the Prince of Wales to find a suitable tutor for his elder son, Edward, to prepare him for entry to Trinity College, Cambridge in the September. The summer of 1883 has always been taken as the first time Stephen met Prince Edward, yet there exists a mysterious photograph of the two princes in Melbourne, taken two years earlier during their Australian stopover from HMS Bacchante. The two princes are shown surrounded by a group of men, and peering through from the back, but central to the photograph is a grinning figure that looks very much like Stephen. It would be typical of him to get into a prominent position. There is no supporting evidence to confirm that this is indeed Stephen, nor to explain how he could have been in Australia, unless he was part of the Bacchante personnel. Records of the crew and camp followers do not mention his name. In 1881 Stephen was at Cambridge and yet......

Stephen was Dalton's suggestion. The choice was apt for in addition to Stephen's personal qualities, his grandfather, Sir James Stephen, had had a similar role. He had been appointed to aid the intellectual progress of the same Prince of Wales. Queen Victoria had realised that her son, and next in line to the throne was not very bright, and she prayed for divine help to bring some normality to his education. He did show an interest in English history and in Napoleon III. It was to Napoleon that the future Prince of Wales said, as they toured Paris together, 'I should like to be your son'. Sir James's role and Stephen's were not quite the same. Sir James's involved a single assessment with recommendations, whereas Stephen was at

Prince Edward's side continuously for three months. Sir James was gloomy in his report 'his power of combination is overtaking the power of extraction with more than usual tardiness'. Whatever this verdict meant, it did not sound encouraging. The employment of Sir James to examine the Prince of Wales was described by Elizabeth Longford as 'a sledgehammer to crack a nut'. An apposite comment however the phrase is interpreted.

The temptation for Stephen to move into the centre of the royal family and to become friends with a future monarch was, not surprisingly, overwhelming. He was to a degree following in family footsteps, and it offered a unique opportunity of incomparable privilege. It also fitted perfectly with the social progress his family had been making for the past hundred years. Stephen's credentials were excellent. His family had a fine record in legal careers, he was an Etonian, a recent successful graduate of Cambridge and he had Dalton's recommendation. Unfortunately no one spotted the recurrent records of 'illness through overwork' which kept cropping up in his family's history. By this time Stephen's own erratic behaviour should have been noticed. Stephen took no persuading to accept the offer to tutor the Prince for three months, and in July 1883 he began work at Sandringham.

The appointment caused great interest amongst Stephen's friends and acquaintances, and was seen not as an interference with his legal studies, but as a predictable ascent into the stratosphere of society. Two people in particular took a close note of his progress. Stephen's guide since the age of nine, Oscar Browning now ensconced at King's, did not view the appointment happily. In fact he was most envious that one of his pupils, and not him, should take this prize. He put it about that Stephen only got the position because 'the official arranging the matter had failed to find me in my rooms'.

The other person to react vigorously was Harry Wilson. Always socially ambitious, he now saw a route, via Stephen, to the royal family. So without delay he set about ingratiating himself with Stephen, as an essential first step. On 14 July as soon as Stephen's post had been announced, he sent him a poem in Greek from his cottage in North Wales. Translated, it ran:

> 'Where have you been? Where are you off to Plato?'
> 'I'm leaving from renowned Athens for Syracuse'
> 'What project are you going to undertake?'
> 'A most worthwhile one, my friend
> I am going to reveal to the city's future tyrant
> Virtue and Eternal Wisdom'

The representations are clear. Wilson compared Stephen to Plato who left Athens (London) to teach in the courts of the powerful rulers of Sicily (Sandringham, Windsor and so on). Especially in the court of Dionysius, the tyrant of Syracuse, where Plato became tutor to his son Dion. Wilson went on to imply that Stephen was ideally suited to teach eternal values to the heir to the throne. The term 'tyrant' was not here derogatory. It was the correct title of the ruler of Syracuse and alluded to the power and influence that position held.

It was a small erudite work of art, all the more impressive for being in Greek, and Stephen cannot fail to have been flattered and impressed. He was literate in Greek to a high standard and was enthusiastic for its study and usage.

It soon became clear to Stephen that his was no easy duty. Like his father, Prince Edward, verged on the backward, and private tutors had failed to give him even a basic grasp of any subject. The Rev. John Dalton who instigated Stephen's appointment had for years struggled with the task, but eventually had to admit 'Prince Eddy fails not in one or two subjects but in all. The abnormal dormant condition of his mind prevents his attention being fixed to any subject for more than a few minutes consecutively'. It was Dalton acting as the Prince's guardian during his training on the naval ship Britannia who, in despair, recommended that the Prince should be sent home because 'his standard of intelligence being too low to make it possible for him to compete with the average cadet'. It was a recommendation that his mother rejected. She blamed Dalton. It had been a condition laid down by the Prince of Wales, that when his son entered Cambridge he would take no examinations, and be awarded an honorary degree. This was a wise move.

Soon after Stephen had taken up residence at Sandringham, he found himself sitting next to the Prince of Wales at dinner. A report of their conversation recalled how 'they discussed the future career of the young Prince at length and in such a manner that Mr Stephen was deeply impressed with the Prince's interest in his son's welfare'. Stephen's natural charm persuaded the Prince that his son's tuition and guidance were safe with him. Stephen suggested that it would be a good idea if the Prince could be introduced to some of the most able men that he would meet at Cambridge, by way of preparation for the university and so that there would be some senior, respected figures with whom the Prince could socialise. The Prince of Wales agreed. It was now that Harry Wilson's aspirations were realised. On 8 August he received a letter from Stephen inviting him to visit Sandringham. It was a tempting invitation. 'Come and stay for a day or two or for a longer time. You would be quite alone all morning, but cricket, lawn tennis, billiards, horses and other instruments of amusement would be within your reach at all times. The other inhabitants will include HRH. He would profit from making your acquaintance. You might meet Goodhart if you come next Saturday'. This was, of course Henry Goodhart, one of Stephen's oldest friends. The other members in the party of six were the Rev. Dalton, a tactful inclusion to give continuity to the Prince's education, the Hon. Patrick Bowes-Lyon, whose father was the Earl of Strathmore, and a naval officer F.B. Henderson who had accompanied the Prince on his long cruises on HMS Bacchante. On arrival, the party was given a tour of Sandringham, inspected the stables and kennels, and then was taken to their accommodation at Bachelors' Cottage on the estate. Stephen described life at Bachelors' Cottage. 'We are six in this little house, a sort of adjunct to the big one in whose grounds it stands, and we lead a quiet and happy reading-party sort of life with all the ordinary rustic pursuits. I have a fat and speedy nag all to myself, and I give him plenty to do'. Others, carefully chosen by Stephen, joined the party including Harry Cust, another Etonian contemporary, and emergent journalist. Cust, noted Wilson, 'is charming'. The mornings were set aside for the Prince's study and in the afternoons and evenings the group met. By all accounts they enjoyed themselves playing billiards, American bowls and cards with the Prince. They encouraged him to talk about his travels. It had been a thoroughly relaxing few days and Stephen had established his proprietorial rights over the Prince, who in return was delighted at the stage management. During the Prince's time at Cambridge it was these people who formed the nucleus of his friends.

Bachelors' Cottage was the place where the three months' tuition took place, and each day the two men met for four hours. The Prince was friendly, enthusiastic and impressionable, and would have been most malleable in Stephen's hands. The closeness and privacy of their relationship did lead to suspicions.

Stephen as he was later to admit had had many 'intimate relationships' with men and there is plenty to suggest that at Eton young boys attracted him. The Prince, who later on was known to frequent gay clubs, could in his naivety, have been happy to be a submissive partner. What the Prince lacked in worldliness he made up with an ambitious sexual drive. It was a drive that certainly included women as well as men. The question is whether the three months with Stephen accounted for his interest in the latter. Whatever the truth during the time that the Prince was at Cambridge, he was a willing vassal of Stephen. Once the Prince left Cambridge, Stephen's influence quickly faded – a change which Stephen did not like.

Whatever progress Stephen made socially as a result of his royal connection, it was not matched by any improvement in the Prince's academic performance. Dalton's long years of frustration meant that he was happy to delegate all tuition to Stephen, although he was careful not to entirely forgo his role of royal intermediary. Stephen had to appear to respect Dalton, and occasionally had to meet his requests. One such request came from the Prince of Wales, via Dalton towards the end of August. It was for a progress report on his son.

Stephen's report was comprehensive, and commendably frank. He was confident enough to eschew the sycophantic, and deferential. The report was dated 30 August 1883, and signed by Stephen. It read:

'Sandringham, Norfolk

In the two months' work, reading on average 4 hours a day, Prince Edward has gone through English history from the beginning down to the end of Edward III's reign. The notes which I have partly written and partly dictated for him extended to the end of Edward I's reign. We have read between two and three hundred pages of each of the books which have formed our regular staple – Bright's History of England, Green's Short History of the English People as well as Langmead's Constitutional History of England. I have taught him, from other books a little about the history of other countries as far as it helped to illustrate that of England, but we have confined ourselves almost entirely to English history and particularly to the history of the English Constitution.

I have not gone on with Mill's Representative Government, which I began to read with him at first. I have confined myself to general remarks on political theories and political terms as I was able to introduce incidentally.

We have done almost all our work by reading aloud. Prince Edward has done a little reading by himself but with very little effect. He has sometimes written answers to questions on what we have read; but this has always been at the cost of a great deal of time and with very little result. I have also tried the experiment of putting my remarks to some extent in the form of a Cambridge lecture and trying to get him to make notes of what I have said. But this was not successful. It is impossible to get him to understand things without much more explanation than a lecturer would every have time to give and his difficulty in finding words to express his meaning – which often prevents him for a long time from answering questions on something that he knows perfectly – is necessarily a great obstacle to his taking notes on what he hears. I do not think he can possibly derive much benefit from attending lectures at Cambridge. He will learn much more by means of private tuition and by this means he may in time acquire enough quickness of mind to be able to be taught in the ordinary way and to read books and write notes or answer to questions without supervision or assistance. But I am sorry to say that this point of development has certainly not been reached yet.

With regard to learning by heart and recitation I thought that it would be better to begin with poetry before coming to prose. Prince Edward learnt some stanzas of Scott and a speech or two from Shakespeare. He learnt so slowly that we had not time for anything more, but I think he speaks the lines very fairly well and with marked improvement in some ways.

We have not got nearly so far in English history as I hoped to do. I found that everything must be gone over a good many times; and I have perhaps made the mistake of going rather too much into detail and spending time over small points of rather slight importance. I hope this is a fault on the right side; because I think the great object is to show Prince Edward how to work hard and methodically and also to provide him with a good many pieces of knowledge about early English history learnt so that he will not forget them.

Prince Edward's one great difficulty is in keeping his attention fixed. He hardly knows the meaning of the word to read. If he uses the grammatical sense of what he is reading, he is quite content without ever realising or trying to realise its actual meaning. In this respect he varies very much from day to day and from hour to hour. Sometimes he attends pretty well for a time, and then suddenly, for no apparent reasons, his mind relapses into a state of torpor.

If this difficulty in keeping his intellectual faculties awake and in concentrating his attention can once be got over, I see no reason why he should not become a tolerable scholar of English history. The subject interests him and he has a very fair memory for the more picturesque parts. We have got through that part of the work which will I think be the most distasteful and difficult to him and I think the deficiency in attention which I have mentioned has perceptibly diminished; though at times it seems as bad as ever.

Sandringham   Aug 30 1883
J.K. Stephen'

It is a remarkable document, perhaps the most comprehensive academic report in existence about a senior member of the royal family and prospective monarch. It reveals the full limitations of the 19 year old Prince. He could scarcely read or write and his attention span was negligible. Stephen's view that 'I do not think he can possibly derive much benefit from attending lectures at Cambridge', underlines the futility of the royal family's plan for the Prince. The report itself was honest, and constructive and just the sort of assessment, albeit very disappointing, that a concerned parent would want. Stephen deserved credit for producing a positive report, respectful yet free of flattery. Perhaps his commitment to the task, and his concern for the Prince's future enabled him to construct such an honest document. It has been suggested in recent times that the Prince was dyslexic, which caused him to appear illiterate, and to have learning difficulties. Other members of contemporary European royal families had the same symptoms. We now know that dyslexia is an inherited condition and can be passed from one generation to another. It will be remembered that the Prince's father was none too literate and seldom read a book.

Fortunately for Stephen, the Prince of Wales took no exception to this rather bleak assessment nor did it have any effect on the Prince's royal progress. There was no malice in Stephen's report. At about the same time, still at Sandringham, he wrote to a friend that the Prince was a 'good natural, unaffected youth, and disposed to exert himself to learn some history'.

On 11 September the London Gazette reported that on 3 September at Balmoral 'the Queen had been graciously pleased to dispense with all statutes and regulations usually observed in regard to installation and grant her Most Gracious Majesty's grandson HRH Prince Albert Victor Christian Edward, Knight of the Most Noble Order and duly invested with the Knight's privileges belonging to a Knight Companion of the Most Noble Order of the Garter'. The Queen obviously saw no need to observe constitutional procedures as far as her eldest grandson was concerned.

So the 'golden weeks' continued at Bachelors' Cottage without interruption until the end of September, then as planned the Prince took up his place at Trinity College. This at least enabled Stephen to claim that the objective of the three months tuition had been achieved, so he could regard his efforts as successful. Bachelors' Cottage still exists. In 1893 the Duke's younger brother, George, married and went to live there. It was renamed York Cottage, and today it serves as the Estate Office, and provides apartments for employees.

Chapter 8

Chaperon to a Prince

One man notable by his absence from the cosy Bachelors' Cottage coterie was Oscar Browning. He was none too pleased at this exclusion, but as soon as the Prince's entourage reached Cambridge he set about putting the matter right. It was Stephen who introduced Browning to the Prince and within days of the start of the term Browning was able to tell his mother 'In the evening I dined at a great feast at Trinity. I was close to the young Prince and had plenty of opportunity of gazing at him. He is nicer looking than his pictures and much like his mother. He has a pleasant good-tempered face, but there is a general agreement that he is not very clever'. Browning would invite the Prince to his room as often as possible on any pretext such as to view a new bathroom. Occasionally he lured him to his 'Sunday Evenings', and delighted in entertaining the Prince by playing one of his several harmoniums. He even attempted a game of hockey in the hope of bumping into the Prince. In the following May he again reported to his mother 'I saw a good deal of him. I found him particularly agreeable'. For Christmas 1884 he presented the Prince with a silver cigarette case. Arthur Benson was another who visited the Prince's rooms whenever he could. He wrote in his diary that the Prince 'was always good-naturedly pleased to see one and Dalton showed me much fatherly kindness'. Dalton described Benson as 'an object of adoration'.

Although Stephen's tuition responsibilities were over he still had a watching brief over the Prince, and to an extent controlled how and with whom he spent his time. It was as if he formed a sort of one man praetorian guard. He introduced the Prince to whist and he became a keen player. The card group, which was organised by Stephen, included himself, Dalton, H.H. Turner, Herbert Stephen and Harry Wilson. The latter also played hockey to impress the Prince. Wilson was determined to build on his Bachelors' Cottage introduction. He frequently put on dinner parties for the Prince. An entry in his diary reads 'dine with hrh, jk studd, hc goodhart, ronald etc to cust's later'. Hrh was the Prince, and the others are easily identifiable – J.E.K. Studd, H.C. Goodhart, Lord Ronald Sutherland Gower and Harry Cust. These were people hand-picked by Stephen and it so happened all had homosexual reputations.

Stephen introduced the Prince to the Amateur Dramatic Society, much to the delight of Oscar Browning who had founded it. The Prince took no active part, but seemed to like 'to patronise performances'. There were plenty of distractions to enable him to enjoy 'the privilege of escaping university examinations, a privilege accorded to his high rank'. The Prince fitted well into the social life of the university. He was known affectionately as 'the Pragga', a Cambridge term for 'Prince'. The Prince's best contribution to the cultural life of the university was when he installed a Bluether concert piano in his rooms. He could not play it, so Stephen arranged for the best piano players in Cambridge to put on small, high standard concerts, led by Professor Stanford, in his rooms. It was unfortunate when the Prince made a particularly tactless remark after a piano recital given by Emil Sauer, a young man of 22 who was staying with Browning. Sauer was full of enthusiasm and delighted to play. Afterwards an over-excited Prince said to Professor Stanford, the University's outstanding pianist – 'Don't you wish you could play like that?'

Another event in the Prince's honour was given by the renown classicist Dr Hugh Munro in December 1883. Munro was the author of a highly regarded poem De Rerum Natura. Fortunately this time the Prince was more discreet and earned a tribute from Harry Wilson 'it was delightful to witness the unaffected courtesy and deference which the Prince displayed to old men and especially to the distinguished scholar who was entertaining him'.

For a while Stephen tried to interest the Prince in the Cambridge Union, of which he had been President a year earlier, but with only moderate success. The Prince 'was fond of attending as a silent member at the Cambridge Union whenever his friends were speaking'. It was clear Stephen went to a great deal of trouble to show his charge as many different facets of Cambridge life as possible, and at the same time make his supervisory role obvious to all. The colleges too honoured the Prince. In March 1884 the professor of Magdalene College gave an elaborate party for him, and a few weeks later his college tutor Joseph Prior 'gave a ball in honour of the Prince, many hundreds of people being present'. Prior was a senior Fellow at Trinity, but Stephen was in a position to suggest the sort of company and entertainment the Prince would most enjoy. Oscar Browning was an old friend of Prior, and it was in Browning's rooms, in late 1884, that Prior was initiated as a Freemason. Browning gave a banquet consisting of sixteen courses and sixteen wines to celebrate the occasion.

The Prince's rooms were on the second floor of Nevile's Court, the most beautiful and interesting part of the college.

They were known as 'attics' and usually housed the more senior dons and scholars. At one end of the rooms was the Wren library and at the other the College Hall. The area was known as the Cloisters, and it was said that Lord Byron had once occupied the same accommodation. It was a quieter area than the vigorous New Court next door. The Prince made little effort to decorate or personalise his rooms, which were small and simply furnished. The only concessions to his position were some framed pictures of his family, some views of Sandringham, and a sketch of H.M.S Bacchante. Stephen's rooms were next door to the Prince's, so he was able to continue his discreet vetting of the Prince's friends. Dalton lived down the corridor. It was to Nevile's Court that the Prince of Wales came to check out some of these friends and their influences on his son. As an undergraduate, the Prince of Wales had lived in a private house in Madingley, on the edge of Cambridge, so his son's accommodation was a shift in royal policy. Wilson (of course) told of 'the pleasure and honour of a short conversation with the Heir to the Throne'. The Prince of Wales was said to be suspicious of his son's apparent increased interest in sex. Nothing momentous came of the visit and the residents could all relax and their lives continued undisturbed.

Even in the holidays the Prince's Cambridge friends would make sure he did not forget them. When the Prince travelled to Heidelberg to spend nine weeks of the summer of 1884 at the university, Stephen and Wilson both wrote to him. Wilson sent a long enigmatic poem, yet it was clear in its flattery. It included references to Henry Goodhart, Harry Cust, Arthur Clough, Arthur Benson and John Dalton, all of whom were very much part of his Cambridge set. It may have been Stephen that he was referring to when he wrote:

'And finally a word we send
To our Philosopher and Friend;
They say he's coming in July –
We hope 'tis true, for verily,
We miss our mine of curious knowledge'

It ended:

'But 'Halt Genug!'. I hear you say,
I've done, and wish my Prince good-day'

Despite the glamorous distraction of chaperoning a future king of England, and the occasional trip abroad, Stephen did not neglect his legal studies. A measure of how seriously he took them is reflected in the fact that in May 1884 he took his final examinations and on 25 June he was called to the Bar. He had been a student member of the Inner Temple since November 1880, and he had attended classes there under the tutelage of Fletcher Moulton, R.B. Haldane and later Northmore Lawrence. It was his intention to practise at the Chancery Bar, and once he was qualified and free to move down to London he took up chambers at Lincoln's Inn. This would have been in the summer of 1885, as he still had royal duties at Cambridge, and he was working towards a Fellowship at King;'s.

With a Fellowship in mind he published a dissertation on 'International Law' at the end of 1884 and followed it up with a thesis on 'Political Science'. It was these two papers that won him a Fellowship at King's College in 1885. These were not conservative, academic papers, but more radical intellectual works, which the College recognised as being valid and meritorious. For Stephen a Fellowship was a major success. 1885 was annus mirabilis for Stephen. He had become a barrister, and with it the expectation of a successful career, his college had awarded him its highest honour and his supervisory role with the Prince, which he had enjoyed so much, was coming to a successful conclusion. No wonder he wrote in one of his verses:

'The world's a jest and joy's a trinket:
I knew that once: but now – I think it'

1885 had begun with the social event of the year. On 8 January the Prince was twenty-one, and a most elaborate party was organised at Sandringham. Naturally Stephen was invited, also his brother Henry, and several other familiar faces from Cambridge. They included Dalton and Harry Wilson. Wilson was so excited the diary entry merited capital letters and breathlessly records 'the gorgeous illuminations, several hundred guests and a crowd of royalties'. He described his room as 'cosy with a large bed' and the Prince 'quite affable'. Wilson had caught the mood. The guest list included all the members of the royal family, with the exception of the Queen, and several representatives of European monarchies, such as Prince Edward of Saxe-Weimer, the Prince of Leininger, Prince and Princess Christian, the Marquis and Marchioness of Lorne and the Duke and Duchess of Edinburgh. For Stephen too it was a wonderful experience. He recorded the day in detail in a letter to his sister Rosamund.

'We are keeping the birthday of our future K (ing) with great splendour. The first ceremony was after breakfast. Breakfast is rather a casual meal, people dropping in as they feel ready and the Royal people having it by themselves. About 11 we were all assembled in the room where Eddie's presents were put out. A most gorgeous display, pieces of plate worth two or three hundred pounds, about 30 splendidly bound volumes of several books which made all the guests hold up their hands astonished that there should be so many books in the world. Lord Rothschild sent a pin with a pink pearl on it, as big as a bean, another sent a walking stick with a large round jewel on which the P (rince)'s initials were emblazoned in diamonds. Next came the presentation of addresses. The Sandringham tenants came first. It was in the Ballroom we stood there. A tenant read a speech and presented the Prince with a silver plate. Eddie read a speech about the example set by papa and his hope that he would follow it. He smiled and shook as many hands as he could get hold of, and shuffled off. Then came Norwich Mayor and Corporation. They had two addresses, one for the Prince of Wales, and one for Eddie. The Prince of Wales read a speech in a very loud firm voice and said he for his part had no higher ambition than to step in the footsteps of his papa, and has tried to do so, especially in the upbringing of his children. Norwich gave P a splendid gold cup. Then came King's Lynn and Eddie read them a first rate speech saying that he had not forgotten the happy days of his boyhood spent within sight of their historic tower. Then came Cambridge. In a sense of pride and humility the address was taken as read. The Mayor (who is an old friend of mine being the proprietor of the theatre where the Ajax was) merely exchanged a copy of his address for a copy of P E's and handed over a present. Then came King's Lynn grammar school, the headmaster and an undermaster and a boy; the boy was last to go, and after grasping the Prince's hand walked backwards in a very impressive way.

Nothing worthy of note happened till lunch; at lunch we all sat at little round tables at which there were four or five. At my table were Colonel A Ellis (an Equerry), the Duchess of Edinburgh, Prince Christian, the Marquis of Lorne, the Duke of Edinburgh, Miss Stonor (a sort of half lady in waiting to the Princess) and your humble servant. I talked a little to the Duchess of Edinburgh, a good-humoured, lively person and drew out the whole illustrious group on the subject of Rome. 'A week in Rome!' said the Duchess of E 'how could you come away at the end of a week?' 'A week in Rome!' said her august husband 'how could you manage to stay so long' 'Rome is spoilt since I used to know it' said Christian. 'However Sir' said I 'they have found a good deal that is interesting to make up for what has been destroyed'. 'Oh' said the Duchess of E 'the Prince means that the cardinals do not chant in the same way that they used to'. 'You did not have a fever', said the Duke 'I can understand your liking to stay'. 'If I had had more time' said I 'I might have stayed more than a week'. And so on. I give you this literally so you may see how like these august people are to us in terms of their conversation at least.

After lunch we all went to a circus at which the whole of the inhabitants of the neighbourhood and school children were invited. It was a good circus. We trooped in on a path marked 'Royal Entrance only'! to the strains of 'God Save the Queen' and among the acclimations of the crowd. On the way I talked to the Marchioness of Lorne – a most attractive person. I could not make out if it was her or not, and I only said Ma'am once and that dutifully. Afterwards I found out who it was.

After the circus I took a walk with Prince Christian and the Marquis of Lorne. It rained and was cold. Post going in a few minutes I must stop. My only prayer for tonight is that I may find a quiet corner at the Ball. We are to wear our fine clothes at dinner too.

Your affectionate brother JKS'

Stephen was revelling in the heady excitement of hob-nobbing with royalty. Outside the immediate royal family he had been placed on the most senior luncheon table with the expectation he would entertain the dignatories with polite conversation. A role he had no trouble in fulfilling. He was also accorded the honour of staying in Sandringham. The less privileged including various Lords, Ladies and Honourables, were put up with the Lieutenant-General Sir Dighton Probyn at Park House. Stephen's letter to his sister is dated 8 January, the day of the party, and all Stephen's journalistic instincts came to the surface. He could not wait to commit to paper what he had witnessed. He must have dashed off the letter between chatting with Prince Christian and the Ball in the evening. He was determined to get the letter into the post that day. No wonder his memory of the lunchtime conversations was so good.

Prime Minister William Gladstone sent a highly respectful letter of congratulations. It included the sentiments:

'Sir, As the oldest amongst the confidential servants of Her Majesty, I cannot allow the anniversary to pass without notice which will tomorrow bring your Royal Highness to full age, and thus mark an important epoch in your life. There lies before your Royal Highness the prospect the occupation – I trust at a distant date – of a throne, which to me at least appears the most illustrious in the world. I fervently desire and pray, and there cannot be a more animating prayer, that your Royal Highness may ever grow in the principles of conduct, and may be adorned with all the qualities, which correspond with this great and noble vocation. Heartily desiring that in the life of your Royal Highness every private and personal may be joined by every public blessing, I have the honour to remain, Sir, your Royal Highness's most dutiful and faithful servant.

W.E. Gladstone'

Gladstone duly received an appropriate reply from the Prince for which he sought permission to release to the press. However,

Gladstone's staff noticed that the grammar of the letter was bordering on the incoherent. The secretary reported 'I found part of it admitted to no possible grammatical construction'. It was not a document that could safely be passed to the papers. Gladstone's secretary, with great tact, went back to the Prince's father and a new draft was agreed. This could then be released. Extracts from the amended version ran as follows:

'Dear Mr Gladstone,

I wish I were better able to answer your very kind letter. Amongst the many offerings, which have reached me, I prize nothing more than the letter you have so kindly written. I assure you the letter shall have the attention, which words from yourself must deserve. It admirably describes, much which demands my most earnest thought on this perhaps the most important birthday of my life.

With my most kind remembrances to Mrs Gladstone, believe me, yours very sincerely,

Albert Victor'

Messages of support and good wishes came from all round the country. The Mayor and Corporation of Windsor sent an address, illuminated on vellum and the Mayor of Norwich gave a children's party in St Andrew's Hall. They were served with buns and oranges. Liverpool City Council sent an address, and the Mayor of Newcastle marked the occasion by setting aside, for immediate distribution, £100 to the poor of that city. In the letter to his sister, Stephen missed recording the main gifts, perhaps because they were delivered in private. These were a silver punchbowl from the Queen, a pair of guns from his father, and a silver cup from both his parents. Amongst other offerings great and small, was a pair of cuff links with diamonds from the Duke and Duchess of Edinburgh, and from the Crown Prince and Princess of Germany a copy of Peter the Great's table at Potsdam. Stephen's own gift to the Prince was an ink stand. The circus to which Stephen referred was provided by Sangers, and was laid on as free entertainment in front of 2000 spectators. No wonder the 250 Sandringham labourers gave a choreographed three cheers. The owner of the circus, John Sanger, described his entertainment as 'A Royal Circus, Hippodrome and Menagerie consisting of the largest, grandest most wonderful amalgamation of the age with a menagerie of the rarest animals from every part of the known globe'. It was certainly the leading circus of its day, and a few years later Sanger's son, 'Lord' John, gave a Royal Command Performance at Windsor Castle before Queen Victoria and her family.

The Grand Ball in the evening was a magnificent occasion attended by 1000 guests. An eight-course dinner was served which moved from oysters, soups, fish and cutlets through to meats, game, puddings and ice cream. Some of the more exotic items were the Puree de Volaille a la Reine, the Turbot sauce Homard, the Aloyau de Boeuf roti and the Canards Sauvages. After such feasting it is hard to see how anyone could fill up an invitation card to twenty dances. On the back of the menu was a 'booking form' for each dance, to be filled in with a lady's name. Amongst the dances on offer were polkas, waltzs, quadrilles, and to end the evening, a gallop. It was not an understated evening in any respect, and may account for Stephen's remark in his letter to his sister that he hoped to find a quiet corner during the Ball. Not surprisingly Wilson records that he had to 'sleep very late' and that breakfast was at noon. All must have been sated and exhausted. However, the pace was unremitting and in the evening the guests were all back for another dinner. It was no less grand than the previous day's although this time the guests were spared the dancing. The same categories of courses were served and this time the highlights were the Puree a la Palestine, the Crepinettes de Foie Gras aux Truffes, the Hanche de Venaison roti, and the Gateaux a la Napolitain. The Prince's coming of age had been properly celebrated. Wilson made one curious comment in his diary that 'james strangely quiet'. This was clearly a reference to Stephen but what brought this uncharacteristic mood on is not known.

In the morning the guests departed. The Cambridge representatives were driven to Norwich station and hence by train home. The Prince completed the pleasure with a Royal meet of the West Norfolk fox hounds. Members of the hunt and their friends were given pre-hunt refreshments, and at midday the hounds arrived. The party made their way to the Commodore Wood, and it was reported that several foxes were despatched. It had been a memorable few days. The Prince recorded his own pleasure in a letter to his cousin Prince Louis of Battenberg. 'We had a really pleasant party. Strange to say, all the relations got on wonderfully well together, and everything went off without a hitch'.

Prince Louis and his wife the Duchess of Fife had not attended the birthday, and perhaps this omission related to a matter involving the actress and society figure Lillie Langtry. In 1880 Louis had taken over from the Prince's father as Langtry's lover. A child was born to them, and the Prince of Wales arranged for a large cheque to be paid to Langtry to sweep the indiscretion under the carpet. The solicitor George Lewis, who worked for both Langtry and the Prince of Wales, and was an expert in concealing royal slip-ups, handled the paperwork.

Chapter 9

An Uncomfortable Transition

Once again Oscar Browning had missed out on a major social occasion, which would have left him angry and frustrated. He was a huge snob and loved nothing more than to be associated with the great and the good. After he was introduced to Emperor Franz Josef of Austria, he remarked 'he was the nicest Emperor I ever met'. For years he tried to establish a genealogical connection with the poet Robert Browning and he employed experts to trace back both families for a common link. He met Browning through a mutual friend and cultivated his friendship at every opportunity. He even managed to visit him twice in Italy. All this effort was to no avail and Browning had finally to admit 'I am reluctantly brought to the conclusion that there is probably no connection between the poet and myself'. He consoled himself 'except the connection of friendship which is often stronger than that of blood'. Browning was happier when Queen Victoria's son Alfred sent him a letter in which he recalled the most pleasant experience of sharing a Turkish bath together. Once when Browning discovered that there was 'only' a Grand Duke waiting for him at his destination in Italy, he instructed his valet to put out his second best dress coat. In his autobiography he listed amongst his friends and acquaintances thirty- seven lords, and two dozen assorted kings, dukes and earls. There was still room for a few cardinals, bishops, admirals and several princes. Yet try as he might he could not break into Prince Edward's inner circle.

Browning's exclusion from the Prince's nearest and dearest did not affect his friendship with Stephen. The two continued to meet and correspond regularly, and two letters from Stephen to Browning, both written in October 1885, still exist. In the letter of the 6th, written from the family's retreat at Anaverna in Ireland, he told Browning that a review of 'D of Leeds in the St J' would be sent to him. It was a review Stephen had requested to write but W H Pollock, the editor, advised him 'it was bespoke for'. Later in the month Stephen, still unable to break his ties with Cambridge, told Browning that 'I am coming to King's for a few days on the 16th and shall no doubt see you'. Three weeks later he wrote again, this time from the Judge's lodgings in Maidstone. He invited Browning to have dinner with him and his father on 7 November at Trinity College and to meet some Apostles. Although Stephen was by now an Angel, he was still entitled to attend Apostle meetings whenever he wished.

Browning continued to live and work at King's until 1908. Then at the age of 70, the College felt he should retire. Again Browning was reluctant to be moved, but the blow was softened by the award of a £300 annual pension. There had been a move to reduce this rather generous amount, but the Provost insisted.

Browning's final vanity took place towards the end of his life when he had retired to Rome. He felt his life deserved a suitable accolade, an official recognition of its value to the nation. He had always kept in touch and remained on good terms with George Curzon. He enjoyed the reflected glory of Curzon's illustrious career. So Browning wrote to Curzon suggesting that a knighthood would be appropriate to mark his work in fostering Anglo-Italian relations. Curzon had just been appointed Foreign Secretary so he was ideally placed to influence a decision. However even nearly fifty years of friendship was not quite enough, and the suggestion was turned down. Perhaps as a consolation prize Curzon did secure for Browning an OBE which, bearing in mind his initials may have an element of compensatory humour. Browning died a year later in 1923, aged 86. He of all people surely deserves the sobriquet 'the last of the camp Victorians'.

A few days after his coming of age, the Prince received an honour, which owed everything to royal privilege. He was entered as a Bencher of the Middle Temple, which made him more senior than the recently qualified Stephen. A note in The Times on 26 January stated that 'Prince Edward of Wales has been entered as a student at the Honourable Society of the Middle Temple, but it is very probably that he will not begin his terms until the ensuing Easter Term in April next. It is also understood that the Prince of Wales who is a Bencher of this Society will dine with the Benchers on the occasion of Prince Edward eating his first dinner in the Hall as a student'. The Prince knew nothing of the law, despite his degree, and had no aspirations for a legal career. Nor would he have sought this honorary bauble.

As the year wore on, Stephen began to spend more time at his chambers at 6 New Square, Lincoln's Inn, which he could easily reach from the family home at 32 De Vere Gardens in Kensington. He was a barrister and had every expectation of being offered briefs, and developing a lucrative living. However despite this important and difficult professional qualification, he never seemed fully committed. He began to spend time writing pieces for the St James's Gazette, which was edited by his father's old friend Frederick Greenwood. Once he wrote a leading article on the train between Paddington and Maidenhead. His poetry was published in several magazines including the Gazette, the Pall Mall Gazette and the Saturday Review. He much preferred to write poetry or prose than to study the piles of legal files that faced him at Lincoln's Inn. He was discovering that his oratory, good looks and charm only accounted for so much. He did not enjoy the painstaking attention to detail. Several of his less talented colleagues at Cambridge had found legal work with government departments, but this too held no attraction. His view of a barrister's lot was summed up in a few lines taken from his verse 'My Education':

> 'At Lincoln's Inn I'd read a brief
> Abstract a title, study
> Great paper piles, beyond belief
> Inelegant and muddy'

Meanwhile the Prince's eighteen months as an undergraduate were drawing to an end. They culminated in a series of dinner parties, and balls that took up most of May. These carefree, summer days were perhaps the happiest of the Prince's life. The last ball of all was at St John's Lodge at the beginning of June. The partygoers had danced all night and now a group of them walked back towards Trinity as the sun came up. Amongst them were the Prince, Stephen, his brother Henry, Harry Wilson and Henry Goodhart. They decided to turn into the Bowling Green and have a last cigar before finally going their separate ways, in some cases for ever. A last photograph was essential and this remarkably still survives today. It showed the Prince surrounded by thirteen friends. Stephen took a prominent central position, directly behind the

Prince. He was wearing a white floppy hat and smoking his trademark pipe. It is noticeable that in group photographs he usually sought to stand out by some element of individuality. Seven of the group were Apostles, which may say something about the sort of people who sought to bind themselves to the Prince, and to whom he was prepared to reciprocate friendship.

Stephen left a lasting impression on Cambridge, both during his time as an undergraduate and as the gatekeeper for Prince Edward. Years later Desmond MacCarthy wrote in 'Portraits', 'when I went up to Cambridge JKS had been dead some years, but his bulky shade still stalked about the colleges and gardens that he loved; still hovered in tobacco smoke when late discussion guttered into reminiscence and wicker chairs creaked drowsily. Laughter still followed the echoes of his ingenious raillery, of his crashing common sense and anecdotes of his wild eccentricities JKS belongs to those dim, romantic, figures who have loomed much greater in intimacy than in performance'. So it was that as 1885 came to an end, Stephen's star had never shone so brightly. He had left a dazzling seven years at Cambridge, become an intimate of royalty and could look forward to a career, which his friends anticipated would mean 'the qualifying age for judges would have to be lowered'. But as the year drew on there were signs that Stephen had not made the transition from Cambridge to the Law Courts in his own mind. He continued to write every two or three weeks to Browning. Sometimes from around the country to where his legal duties had taken him. He found time in December to write a long poem for the Literary and Scientific Society dedicated to Arthur Clough. It appeared in the Etonian, and although his friend Robert Pashley had been dead a few years, he was remembered. Stephen was failing to move on in his life.

When Stephen took up residence in Lincoln's Inn he found himself surrounded by old friends, or people from similar backgrounds. His brothers Herbert and Henry were there. Herbert was at 4 Paper Buildings and just opposite was Henry at 3 King's Bench Walk. Three doors away from Henry at No 9 was a man called Montague Druitt who was to become significant in Stephen's life. He was from a distinguished medical family in Wimborne in Dorset, and had been educated at Winchester College and New College, Oxford. His disciplines were classics and the law. His background was therefore similar to Stephen's, and as both arrived at Lincoln's Inn at about the same time, it was natural that their paths would cross, and that they would become friends. For a while Druitt taught at a boarding school in Blackheath to fund his legal studies, and to maintain chambers at Lincoln's Inn. In Harry Wilson's diary, a John Henry Lonsdale is mentioned. Lonsdale's home address was within a stone's throw of the school where Druitt taught, and when Lonsdale came to Lincoln's Inn his address was 4 King's Bench Walk. When Lonsdale left the law for the church in 1887 he was appointed curate at Wimborne Minster. The suggestion is that Druitt used his local family influence to secure Lonsdale such a prestigious first appointment. Another example of the cliquishness of Lincoln's Inn was that sharing rooms at 9 King's Bench Walk with Druitt was Reginald Brodie Dyke Acland, like Druitt a Wykehamist and the brother of Sir William Gull's son-in-law. Gull was one of Queen Victoria's doctors, and was also the family physician for the Stephen family. Another solicitor who shared No 9 was Edward Bedford, and it was he who was centrally involved in covering up a particularly nasty social scandal, known as the Cleveland Street Affair in 1889. This was a matter which was to engulf Prince Edward, and indirectly have unwelcome consequences for Stephen.

1. 15 Sunderland Terrace, W2 – the birthplace of Stephen (*A.A. Leighton*)

2. Stephen attended Park House School, near Tonbridge, for one year at the age of 8 (*Southborough Society*)

3. Stephen's family home was at No. 32 De Vere Gardens, far down on the right hand side (*Royal Borough of Kensington and Chelsea*)

4. A bust of Sir James Stephen, Stephen's grandfather, by Carlo Marochetti (© *National Portrait Gallery, London*)

5. A drawing by G.F. Watts of Stephen's father, Sir James Fitzjames Stephen (© *National Portrait Gallery, London*)

COLLEGERS ELEVEN, 1877
C.W. Chitty   C.M. Smith   C.A. Spring-Rice   F.H.C. Wellesley   T.H. French   H.P. Hawkins
A.L. Mumm   R.H. Macaulay   J.K. Stephen   B. Farrer   P. Bridges

6. The Collegers' Eleven, captained by Stephen, that contested the Eton
Wall Game in 1877 (*Provost and Fellows of Eton College*)

7. James John Hornby, the
headmaster of Eton throughout
Stephen's time there (*Provost and
Fellows of Eton College*)

8. A.C. (Arthur) Benson, a friend
and admirer of Stephen at Eton
and Cambridge (*Provost and
Fellows of Eton College*)

9. A photograph of George Curzon (later Lord) and Oscar Browning taken on holiday in Milan 1878 (*John Lane, London*)

10. King's College, Cambridge as it was in Stephen's time (*Provost and Scholars of King's College, Cambridge*)

11. The Cambridge production of *Ajax* with Stephen in the lead role
(*John Swain*)

Hugh Benson
Gerald Duckworth   M. Sanderson   J.K. Stephen   Walter Crum   Walter Headlam
E.L. Sanderson   E.F. Benson   M.R. James   E.H. Douty   Marcus Dimsdale   R. Carr Bosanquet

12. A group of T.A.F. club members, including Stephen, and several other
noted intellectuals (*Gary A. Brown*)

13. The Savile Club, where Stephen was a member at its then premises in Piccadilly (*The Savile Club*)

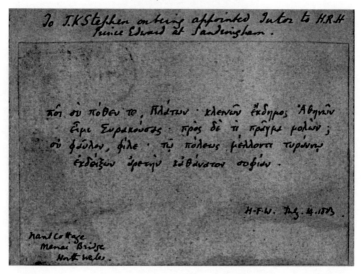

14. Harry Wilson's poem sent to Stephen to mark his appointment as tutor to Prince Edward (*The Royal Archives*)

The Duke of Clarence surrounded by a group of his friends. Seven of the group were Apostles. Standing: J.N. Langley; top row, from left: A.H. Clough, J.K. Stephen, C.V. Stanford; seated, from left: H.B. Smith, J.N. Dalton, F.B. Winthrop, J.D. Duff, H.F. Wilson, J.W. Clark, Prince Edward, H.C. Goodhart, H.L. Stephen, A.H. Smith

15. Stephen with a group of friends at Cambridge, including his brother Henry, and Prince Edward (*The Royal Archives*)

16. Montague Druitt, a close friend of Stephen, who was also involved in the *Jack the Ripper* story (*Provost and Fellows of Winchester College*)

17. Bachelors' Cottage on the Sandringham estate, where Stephen tutored Prince Edward (*Sandringham Estates*)

SANDRINGHAM.

DINER DU 8: JANVIER. 1885.

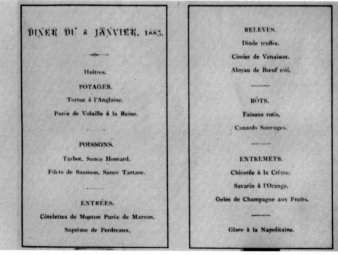

DINER DU 8 JANVIER, 1885.

Huîtres.

POTAGES.

Tortue à l'Anglaise.

Purée de Volaille à la Reine.

POISSONS.

Turbot, Sauce Homard.

Filets de Saumon, Sauce Tartare.

ENTRÉES.

Côtelettes de Mouton Purée de Marron.

Suprême de Perdreaux.

RELEVES.

Dinde truffée.

Cimier de Venaison.

Aloyau de Bœuf rôti.

RÔTS.

Faisans rotis,

Canards Sauvages.

ENTREMETS.

Chicorée à la Crème.

Savarin à l'Orange.

Gelée de Champagne aux Fruits.

Glace à la Napolitaine.

18. The menu for the dinner marking Prince Edward's 21st birthday, which Stephen attended (*David and Pamela MᶜCleave*)

Besides Henry and Herbert Stephen, there were other colleagues from Cambridge days, such as Harry Wilson and Patrick Bowes-Lyon, but the grip Stephen had had on the social life there was slipping. On the surface he was broadening his set of amiable friends but the new environment was more professional and less ephemeral. There was now not so much time for the superficial and amusing. Stephen's social life continued to be enjoyable, but he was being left behind by colleagues who realised that they had competitive careers to follow. Prince Edward too had moved on to concentrate on an army life, and to fulfil royal duties. Stephen was beginning to find himself no longer the centre of attraction.

When Harry Wilson left Cambridge in the summer of 1885 taking with him the accolades of First Bell's Scholar, the Chancellor's Gold Medal for English verse and a First Class in the Classical Tripos, he had no intention of letting slip the introduction to royalty that Stephen had given him at Bachelors' Cottage. Since Prince Edward was busy elsewhere and he himself was working on his law examinations it was difficult for him to arrange meetings. So Wilson's approach was to correspond regularly, usually to invite the Prince to a suitable function or to send him a flattering piece of poetry.

Early in February 1886 Wilson wrote to the Prince to invite him to become President of the newly formed Hockey Association. At Cambridge hockey had been one of the few games that had interested the Prince and which he played with any regularity. The invitation was accepted with enthusiasm. 'You must let the Association know that I was extremely flattered by their wishing to make me President of the Association, which I am now able to accept. I always did as you know, take a great interest in the game of hockey and think it an excellent idea to start an Association'. Later in the letter he wistfully recalled his time at Cambridge and his admiration for Stephen. He said 'I daresay you regret leaving Cambridge, in some ways, as much as I do, as I think, taking it all round, we had a very delightful time there, and the two years spent there went by like lightening [sic]. I hope old Jim Stephen is very flourishing, and I have no doubt he is doing well, as a better man never existed'. High praise indeed from one who was next but one in line for the throne.

A few days later, encouraged by this response, Wilson invited the Prince to attend a performance of Twelfth Night given by the Oxford University Dramatic Club. Writing from the South Cavalry Barracks at Aldershot on 18 February, the Prince replied:

'My dear Harry,

Many thanks for your letter, which I was very glad to get. I should have liked very much to have gone down to Oxford and see the 'Twelfth Night' as you suggest, but I am afraid it is impossible just now, as I have so much to do, and I am not able to get away much except on special occasions. I suppose you will not be able to go down to Cambridge for the opening of the New Union Buildings, but I trust I shall see you again some time. If you would care about it you might come down here sometime during the spring or summer and see what sort of a life I lead here, as I could easily put you up. Excuse this short scrawl, but I am rather hurried today, being on duty.

Ever yours, very sincerely, Edward'

In early May, some verses about the Home Rule Bill winged their way to the South Cavalry Barracks, and it seems a suggestion that he, Wilson, would like to take the Prince up on his offer of a visit to Aldershot. Politely, even apologetically, the Prince regretted that such a meeting was not possible at the moment 'as I am off to town tomorrow for the Derby and shall be away nearly all the week. I hope you will not be disappointed. I thought the poems you sent me were very good, and they certainly do you great credit as they are only too true'.

Meanwhile Stephen was busy at Lincoln's Inn, trying to convince himself that in view of his father's enthusiasm he should follow in his legal footsteps. He moved from his chambers to 6 New Square. Why he did so and who were the principal tenants is not known since records of such details were not kept. This was because New Square did not belong to the Inn, and to this day the Inn has never been the sole proprietor of New Square even though it is within its precincts. What is known is that Stephen at this stage was described as an equity draughtsman and conveyancer.

It was about this time that another of Stephen's weaknesses began to show itself, an inability to handle or appreciate money. He had become too used to his father subsidising him at every turn and he was unwilling to realise that he, as a barrister, should be responsible for his own finances. His earnings as a draughtsman and conveyancer would not have amounted to much and merely to be at Lincoln's Inn incurred costs. There were legal fees, subscriptions and an obligatory number of dinners to attend and to be paid for. The wine bill alone would have been substantial. He would have done well to note the approach of his friend Montague Druitt who had worked as a schoolmaster and done relatively menial legal work as a special pleader to support himself. Nor was Druitt a drain on his family as his board and lodgings were covered by the school. In contrast Stephen continued to live free at home at De Vere Gardens, and from later correspondence we know that he received an allowance each year of £500. He was failing to make the switch between academic life, and the independent commercial world. It was a switch he never completely made, and to an extent it must be attributed to an uninterrupted early life of success and adulation.

Stephen had always had a hankering for the literary world, and it was this that diluted his commitment to legal matters. He had begun to contribute to St James's Gazette in 1884 and during the second half of 1886 his output increased. A little later Oscar Wilde started to write to the Gazette. It was usually to express dissatisfaction with reviews of his work as in the case of 'The Picture of Dorian Gray'. Sometimes he would attack the Gazette itself for publishing such criticism. He described the Gazette as 'seeking apparently to be the organ of the prurient, which sees or pretends to see in it [Dorian Gray] all kinds of dreadful things and hints at Treasury prosecutions'. The fact that Wilde felt it necessary to attack the Gazette in such high dudgeon underlined the status and influence the journal enjoyed as a serious, well respected publication. It was a vehicle for views on any topical matter of the day. At about the same time Stephen submitted articles to the Pall Mall Gazette, encouraged by his old friend Harry Cust, who was now the editor. Stephen continued to send in features, reviews and verse from time to time over the next two years. That Stephen was a valued contributor to these two august publications suggested that he was right to believe he had more of a literary future than a legal one.

In 1881, Stephen's uncle Leslie had been on one of his 'Sunday Tramps' walking tours in Cornwall when he came across St Ives 'at the very toenail of England'. Such was his enthusiasm for the town and the surrounding countryside, that the following year he bought Talland House, a large white villa built some forty years earlier. It was within sound of the sea, and had wonderful views across the bay. Leslie Stephen and his wife Julia were the parents of Vanessa and Virginia, (by marriage, Bell and Woolf respectively). They were two of the brightest stars in what became known as the Bloomsbury Set at the beginning of the 20th century. Stephen was therefore a cousin to both of them. When Virginia wrote her celebrated novel 'To the Lighthouse', she based Mr Ramsey's house on Talland. Besides the grandeur of the house itself, Talland had extensive lawns, shrubberies and exotic plants, a grape house, and a plethora of bird life. It also had a private path that led directly to the beach. All this made Talland House a magnet to the Stephen family, particularly the children and Stephen would join the annual exodus from London. There was even a cricket pitch in the grounds and this was regularly used by all concerned. Virginia was a particularly enthusiastic bowler. When she was nine her brother Thoby said of her 'Gin can bowl a good deal better than some of the chaps who came this term'. It is not recorded whether Stephen joined in the cricket but he certainly visited Talland several times and he knew Virginia from her birth in 1882, as well as all the other members of the extended Stephen family.

Talland House was not just a family holiday resort. It became a summer venue for many of the artistic and literary talents of the day, including the painter Walter Sickert and Henry James. James moved next door to the Stephen's London home in 1886. Today a commemorative plaque marks his house at 34 De Vere Gardens, Kensington. Whilst at Talland House, Sickert painted his first known picture 'On the Sands, St Ives'. Unusually it was signed with his first name in full, rather than just an initial. Sickert was the same age as Stephen, and they were just two of the emerging talents to make their way to Talland House. There exists at King's College, Cambridge, a sketch of Stephen that may possibly have been done by Sickert at St Ives in 1884. It was during these holidays that Stephen's first interest in painting was aroused.

Another frequent visitor to Talland House was Walter Headlam. He was seven years younger than Stephen and was introduced to the family by Julia Stephen, who invited him to Cornwall in the mid-1880s. He was educated at Harrow, and King's Cambridge where be became an outstanding Greek scholar and a Fellow of the college. He was part of a group of professional academics who inhabited a world of letters, poetry and classical literature and epigrams. He remained at Cambridge until he died. Julia's daughter Virginia was much taken by his intellect and eccentricity, and she would send her early writings to Headlam for 'sober criticism'. Her sister Vanessa was less sure of Headlam's intentions and was suspicious that Headlam's real motive was to be in the company of young girls. Headlam did make advances to Stella Duckworth, but the interest was not returned. Stella Duckworth was the daughter of Julia by her first marriage to Herbert Duckworth, and the sister of George and Gerald. A few years later at St Ives, Stella recorded that Headlam made similar overtures to her mother Julia. His relationship with Virginia was probably more intellectual than sexual.

Headlam first met Stephen when he became a member of the TAF Club, and clearly held the older man in great awe. He was a founder member of Stephen's Walpole Society, and belonged to the Chitchat Club, although he never progressed to the Apostles. When Stephen died Headlam wrote a sad tribute in verse, and a year later on the anniversary, he composed a long poem of over a hundred lines still mourning the loss in such emotional and elegiac terms that the work bordered on an expression of lost love. Both poems were published in the Cambridge Review.

Talland House and its gardens were something of a paradise of fun, adventure and exploration, and the stimulation of imagination both for children and adults. Eventually the dream had to come to an end. Leslie Stephen was becoming concerned at the cost of running the house, and his two sons, Thoby and Adrian were due to enter public school. He was even worried that the main boiler was about to blow up and injure the servants, which would involve him in further costs. The era at Talland House had been a delight, and several of the beneficiaries were never so happy again.

Chapter 10

Thwarted Ambitions

The year 1886 ended with a bang for Stephen – a nasty bang to the head. It was a blow from which he may never have fully recovered and is often blamed for his eventual sad and premature death. The incident happened when Stephen was making a New Year visit to stay with his friend Felix Cobbold at the family home, The Lodge, in Felixstowe. Felix was the son of Lord Cobbold, the head of a wealthy banking and brewing family, which continued to have great influence and popularity in Suffolk for the next hundred years. Felix Cobbold was one of the main participants in a series of parties that would begin pre-Christmas at King's and then move on to Felixstowe for the New Year. Invitations to The Lodge were highly prized and the generosity of the hospitality, legendary. Golf always featured in the programme and was played at the local Felixstowe club where Arthur Balfour was captain in 1889. The Cobbold family sustained this reputation throughout the 20th century.

On 29 December Stephen was riding along a coastal path, which after a while took him to Walton Mill. Here he stopped to look at a steam engine, which worked the mill and to talk to the mill owner John Bloomfield, when the lookout man blew his whistle to warn of an approaching train. The sound of the whistle frightened Stephen's horse, which reared up and threw Stephen to the ground, leaving him unconscious. The injuries to his head were severe, and although he was patched up by a local doctor, and according to Michael Harrison in his book 'Clarence', he was seen by Sir William Gull as soon as he reurned to London. Gull was one of the leading doctors of the period. Amongst his clients he included Queen Victoria and the Stephen family, and he was to be a key and enigmatic figure in the appalling events which were to envelop the East End of London two years later. Gull's speciality was disorders of the brain and head injuries, so he would have been the correct person to treat Stephen. It has to be said that there is no evidence in the form of medical notes or reports to collaborate Harrison's claim that Gull did actually treat Stephen. Yet several other writers have repeated this view. It was about this time that Gull was gradually gaining the reputation for diagnosing problems and for carrying out treatments which were sometimes polically and socially motivated. According to Harrison, Gull kept a careful check on Stephen, and it was not long before he declared Stephen to be fully recovered. Some years later this was disputed by Stephen's uncle, Leslie Stephen, who wrote of the accident 'the effects were far more serious than appeared at the time. He returned to work before long, but is was noticed that for sometime he seemed to have lost his usual ease in composition' Herbert, Stephen's older brother, was similarly sceptical 'He was badly cut. The wound healed, but I do not think he ever enjoyed perfect health again'. Stephen's friend and admirer Arthur Benson, had the view that Stephen 'began to form sanguine and unbalanced plans, to be extravagent in money matters, and to display emotional tendencies of a rather vehement type? Benson had spoken at the time of 'some subtle inflammation of brain tissue'. It seems the combined views of these three laymen may have been nearer the mark than the optimistic 'complete recovery' allegedly expressed by the celebrated Dr Gull. It does seem likely that the accident accentuated a pattern of erratic and eccentric behaviour that could have been traced throughout his life prior to the fall. This would include temper tantrums as a child, outbursts of bad language and later, mood swings and occasional manic behaviour. There were also all kinds of eccentricities, which at the time could mostly be laughed off. An accident of this type was exactly what he did not need to maintain a semblance of long-term mental equilibrium.

Having recovered, at least partially from this accident, Stephen returned to New Square in Lincoln's Inn, and to his writings for the St James's Gazette. On the surface he seemed none the worse for his experience, but every now and then there were disturbing signs. One of the first to notice was his cousin Virginia Woolf, then aged five. Years later she recalled how he once came rushing wildly into her nursery at 22 Hyde Park Gate in Kensington, waving a swordstick which he thrust into a loaf of bread. She feared his physical presence, his deep blue penetrating eyes, heavy build, and theatrically deep voice. His behaviour and appearance terrified her. She remembered his mad laughter which in retrospect she realised was not normal. She likened him to 'some tormented bull'. Sometimes he would read poetry to her and her sister, from Charles Wolfe's 'The Burial of Sir John Moore'. A subject hardly appropriate for young children. Later on there were other incidents of an even more sinister and unbalanced nature. It was unfortunate that Virginia's home was only about two minutes walk round the corner from Stephen's address.

It was in 1887 that Stephen was invited to join the Committee of the Social and Political Education League, by Judge Fossett Lock, and to be its secretary. Stephen would have been flattered by the invitation coming from such a eminent source, whose background was the same as his, namely Eton and King's College, Cambridge. Lock was about twelve years older than Stephen. The League was a powerful force for helping to improve the lives of the less well off and it was to last well into the 20th century. Lock was its Chairman from 1887 to 1913. A letter written by Stephen on the League's behalf still exists. It was sent from his chambers at 3 Stone Buildings in Lincoln's Inn to lecturers of the League asking them to attend a meeting at 30 Queen's Square, also in Lincoln's Inn on Wednesday 18 May at 5.30 pm. It was handwritten, and signed J K Stephen Hon. Sec. S P E L. No more is known of Stephen's involvement, but Lock went on to become a leading social reformer. He was chairman of the Legal Aid Society, and wrote articles and pamphlets on the Defence of the Poor Prisoners, and Legal Aid for the Poor. Their shared background, and profession, and the easy access to each other in Lincoln's Inn, may explain Lock's choice of Stephen. It may also have helped that Lock knew Leslie Stephen well, and he was a member of the 'Sunday Tramps' brigade.

It was about this time that Stephen may have attempted his first relationship with a woman, when he is supposed to have had an affair, real or imagined, with Eleanor Locker. She was between marriages, firstly to Alfred Tennyson's son, Lionel, who died at sea on holiday in 1885, and secondly to Augustine Birrell who she married in the summer of 1888. Her reputation was for the unconventional and glamorous, and it was this combination that may have led Stephen into one of his extravagant enthusiasms. Eleanor's engagement to Birrell, a lawyer and later a QC was announced in the April, and if there is truth in the story, it would have left Stephen devastated and depressed.

Stephen's real ambition was to found and run his own

journal. It had been apparent since his time at Eton that it was in the literary world that he wished to work, and on 1 January 1888 he realised that dream. Perhaps carried away with the moment he introduced The Reflector with a panache that was both contrived and inaccurate. 'It was recently pointed out that on New Year's Day, 1588, England was thrilled with excitement at the prospect of a Spanish invasion; that on New Year's Day, 1688, the revolution was more or less imminent; that on New Year's Day 1788, appeared the first number of The Times. Well, on New Year's Day 1888, appeared the first number of at least one newspaper'. Unfortunately the first edition of The Times came out on 1 January 1785, and it is most doubtful if 'England was thrilled with excitement at the prospect of a Spanish invasion'.

The name itself may not have been original since a generation earlier two Kingsmen, a Mr Bendyshe and the Provost of King's Richard Okes had edited a paper called The Reflector. Bendyshe was a man of very bad language, and such outrageous ideas that sometimes the printers refused to set up the copy. Predictably the paper soon self-destructed. The aim of Stephen's Reflector was to supply lively criticism of current thought and literature and to be based on one or two main articles. Alas, after seventeen weekly issues Stephen was forced to close it down on 21 April. The reason for its demise was Stephen's lack of financial and business acumen. He ran it as a glorified school magazine with little attention to balancing the books. The talent that The Reflector attracted in its short life was impressive. Names such as George Meredith, Edmund Gosse, Alfred Perceval Graves, Bernard Holland, Leonard Huxley and Leslie Stephen were significant writers of the day. Stephen wrote about half of each edition with great energy and enthusiasm. Occasionally he may have fallen into the editor's trap of expressing personal views, too often and for using The Reflector as a vehicle for putting forward his own opinions, sometimes in verse, a shade self-indulgently. Two poems, which he published in the January demonstrated this. Stephen was always a keen pipe smoker and his work 'The Grand Old Pipe' managed to mix this enthusiasm with a political message on a subject controversial at the time. An extract from it ran:

> 'My pipe was my one consolation
> When its antitype kindled the flame
> Which threatened the brave population
> Of Ulster with ruin and shame
> I forgot that our ruler was dealing
> With scamps of the Sheridan type
> While the true orange colour was stealing
> O'er the face of my Grand Old Pipe'

Another verse, expressed in a jaunty, light-hearted style, conveys Stephen's observations on drinking. It suggests that Stephen recognised the dangers of excess and that amongst his problems this was not one of them. The poem is called 'Drinking Song', and was written for 'A S'. This may have been Archibald Smith, a contemporary of Stephen at Eton. The first and last verses were as follows:

> 'There are people, I know, to be found
> Who say and apparently think
> That sorrow and care may be drowned
> By a timely consumption of drink
>
> For myself, I have managed to do
> Without recourse to this plan,
> So I can't write a poem for you,
> And you'd better get someone who can'

Not that Stephen was abstemious. In a verse for the Pall Mall Gazette dedicated to C S Calverley, he combines the pleasure of a drink and a smoke:

> 'Whene'er I take my pint of beer a day
> I gaze into my glass and think of thee
> When smoking, after lunch is cleared away,
> Thy face amid the cloud I seem to see'

If anything The Reflector attracted an excess of talent, and Stephen was reluctant to select from so much good work. Consequently the paper became too bulky. At the start Stephen had promised sixteen pages in each edition, but sometimes this expanded to thirty-two. Nevertheless Stephen continued to take an 'inexplicably sanguine view of the pecuniary side of the enterprise'. It may also have become too intellectual and circulation never exceeded 250. Its price was 6d (3p), or 7/- (35p) for a quarterly subscription or £1 7s (£1.35) for an annual one. The first sign that the magazine was in trouble may have been evident in late March. On the 18th notices inviting subscribers to renew quarterly payments were sent out. Response was poor, and even Stephen had to realise it was going to be impossible to continue. He accepted the responsibility that if the magazine ceased he would have to reimburse annual subscribers for outstanding copies. Stephen's father had to come to the rescue to settle the debts. If Stephen was casual with money he might have been consoled by the words of one of his heroes, William Wordsworth.

> 'High heaven rejects the lore
> Of nicely calculated less or more'.

In the editorial for the last Reflector, Stephen was coy about the reasons for its demise. He teased the readers with some speculative thoughts. Perhaps he had made his fortune from seventeen issues; perhaps he had had a row with the publisher; perhaps he was stopping when costs and income were the same; perhaps he was already exhausted by his efforts. And so on. The suggestion that came nearest to the truth was the sentence 'although not a ruined man, fearful of sheriffs' officers, and apt to toy significantly with deadly weapons in hours of solitary despondency, I am, nevertheless aware that the limit of expenditure which I am willing to incur is within measurable distance, and that I prefer instant death while my proportions are still bulky and my printing and paper beyond reproach, to the horrors of a lingering end, heralded by increasing leanness and sordid economies'. There may be a clue to Stephen's real feelings in the apparently innocent remark that he 'might crop up at Kensal Green or Crystal Palace'. The magazine was printed at Crystal Palace, and Kensal Green was the site of the family graveyard. Stephen even tried to claim that there had been twenty-eight editions. He reckoned that because he had published 408 pages altogether and some special covers, and because he had originally promised sixteen pages per edition, this represented twenty-eight issues. It was a whimsical piece of arithmetic. Stephen's last wish, as enigmatic and grandiose as ever, was that 'out of the ashes of the dead Reflector may arise a marriage, a murder, or the regeneration of mankind'

Stephen felt this failure very keenly, coming as it did at the same time as news of Eleanor Locker's engagement. Mentally it was a huge blow which would have compounded any physical damage done by his accident at Felixstowe. He attributed events not to his own management, but as a reflection of a philistine society. On 22 April, the day after closure he wrote sadly to

Oscar Browning on specially printed Reflector writing paper bearing the address Lonsdale Chambers, 27 Chancery Lane:

'Dear O B

I have ordered the last four numbers of The Reflector to be sent to you and I regret to add that they are absolutely the four last as I have determined to discontinue its publication. I therefore send back to your cheque for £1, and will you send 2s/2d (11p) instead.

Yours J K S'

Still Stephen could not bring himself to recognise his own shortcomings. He told his father, now a Judge of the Queen's Bench that 'he now wished to dedicate himself entirely to literature'. Meanwhile Harry Wilson was continuing to cultivate his friendship with Prince Edward. His letters always contained the hope that they would meet, and in February 1888 he invited the Prince to watch the Boat Race from his house at Chiswick. The Prince replied:

'Dear Harry,

I was very glad to hear from you again and it is very good of you to think of asking me to come to your place to see the boat-race from. I should be delighted to do so, for it would be very nice to meet some of our old Cambridge friends again whom I have not seem for a long while. But the question is whether I shall be in town then or not at the end of March, for if I am not I fear I shall be detained at York then by my duties with my regiment. But I had better let you know again for certain a little later on, if that would be the same to you.

Ever yours, very sincerely Edward'

Just before the race the Prince wrote to Wilson again on 26 March, this time confirming his unavailability:

'My dear Harry,

I put off writing to you before in the hope of still being able to give a favourable answer. But I now find, very much to my regret, that I shall not be able to get away for next Saturday which is very tiresome for I should have much enjoyed paying you a visit at Chiswick and seeing some of my old friends again. I hope at any rate you will have a pleasant day for it, and I shall think of you all when the time comes.

Ever yours Edward'

Wilson had been thwarted again in his attempt to lure the Prince. The 'house at Chiswick' needs some explanation. It was called The Osiers and was a delightful building with a garden that led down to the Thames. It was also a club of dubious reputation, known as 'a chummery', a word used by those on colonial service in India to mean bachelor quarters. There lies the key of its true purpose. It was a homosexual club catering for the aristocracy, the wealthy, and those sociably well connected. Gentlemen of a certain status were welcome to drop in for an evening, and perhaps stay the night. The club was owned by Harry Wilson, and it was at his instigation that invitations were sent out, and callers vetted for suitability. It may have been The Osiers to which Queen Victoria was referring when she wrote to her grandson expressing her disapproval of parties at a house in Chiswick. 'There is a great fear lest you should have gay parties at Chiswick'. Her choice of words may have been unwittingly most accurate in parlance some hundred years ahead of its   time. The Queen clearly had doubts about her grandson's behaviour and gullibility for she wrote again to him soon afterwards with this warning. 'Avoid the many temptations which beset all young men and especially Princes. Beware of flatterers, too great a love of amusement, of races and betting and playing high. Society is very bad in these days'.

That Wilson was so eager to invite the Prince to The Osiers, says something about the latter's known sexual ambivalence. It would seem certain that Stephen would have been amongst the Boat Race welcoming committee for the Prince. He was a long term friend of Wilson, and it would be most surprising if a gathering of old Cambridge friends for the Prince did not include his old tutor for whom the Prince had such high regard. It is known that from time to time Stephen visited the club and held literary soirees there. Wilson however was nothing if not persistent. A few months later in early June, the Prince was conferred at Cambridge with his honorary law degree, described as an 'honoris causa', probably to dignify this gratuitous award and to impress the nation's non-classicists. Wilson duly sent a lengthy unctuous ode offering fulsome congratulations. It recalls the happy days at Trinity College:

> 'Five years ago – we rode, we read,
> Boated, played hockey, whist, la crosse
> Listened to Seeley, laughed with Gosse,
> And went at shocking hours to bed.
> O days of gold! O sunny prime
> Wherewith no season may compare!'

Wilson ends the eight verses with a stirring trumpet voluntary:

> 'Upon that great, that glorious aim!
> And like her Edwards Third and First
> May you, for England's weal athirst
> Add lustre to a royal name'

The exclusion of Edward II from the verse is significant. He was an ardent homosexual who was murdered on the orders of his wife allegedly by having a burning stake thrust up his backside in Berkeley Castle in 1327. Wilson had done his homework. The investiture ceremony itself owed more to a Gilbert and Sullivan opera than a serious state occasion. The university felt obliged to award the Prince its highest law degree, an LL D since 'Cambridge had been honoured by his presence'. Further it took place on 8 June, which was a special day at Cambridge, known as 'Scarlet Day'. In addition to all the immediate members of the Prince's family there was an array of senior politicians, peers, and service personnel, including 'that political star of eccentric orbit', Randolph Churchill. The Earl of Rosebery, Arthur Balfour, the Marquis of Salisbury, and the Postmaster-General also attended. Afterwards there was a reception in the Master's Lodge and dinner was taken in the Hall at Trinity. A thoroughly enjoyable, meaningless day was had by all. It is surprising that a ceremony of such apparent importance had been delayed three years from the time the Prince left Cambridge. Nevertheless, true to form, Harry Wilson came up with a characteristic poem:

> 'Five years ago. And yet to me
> It seems as if 'twere yesterday
> And I am now a staid MA
> And you, Sir, are an LL D'

A few days after the Prince's academic ties with Cambridge were finally severed his military career received a boost. He was promoted to lieutenant in the 10th Hussars, a cavalry regiment much favoured by royalty and the aristocracy. From now on he was to combine an army life with a programme of rather dull royal duties, such as opening the new Hammersmith Bridge, and the Royal Victoria hospital in Burnley, and attending City functions.

One of the side effects of Stephen's obsession with The Reflector was that he did no legal work at all for four months. His chambers were used as an office to write and publish his newspaper. Its failure was not only a humiliation for Stephen, but of desperate concern to his father who was now aware that his son's career whether in law or literature was coming off the rails. Having provided Stephen with an enviable education, annual allowances, and bank rolling The Reflector's debts, he was wondering how much more support he could give him. In a last attempt to save his son's legal career he appointed him in June 1888 Clerk of Assize for the South Wales circuit. Sir James felt that these relatively light duties would still give his son time to contribute articles to newspapers and might resurrect his interest in the Bar. Apart from trying to help his son, as he thought, there were personal motives in the appointment. His great friend Henry Maine died on 3 February that year, and as a tribute to him he appointed one of Maine's sons to the Clerkship of South Wales. However within a few weeks he too was dead, and now Sir James felt it doubly appropriate to let his own son fill the vacancy. He was keeping the post 'within the family'. Sir James's long relationship with Maine was not above suspicion. He wrote of 'a brotherly intimacy of forty years, never interrupted by a passing cloud'. Of their time at Cambridge Sir James said of Maine 'He was perfectly charming to me at college as he is now. He was most kind, friendly and unassuming, and though I was a freshman and he a young don and he was 26 when I was 20 – one of the greatest differences of age and rank which can exist between two people having so much in common – we were always really and effectually equal.

We have been the closest of friends all through life'. Henry Maine proposed Sir James for membership of the Apostles during his first term at Cambridge and he was elected on 13 November 1847. The nature of their friendship at any rate in the early days is clear, and they remained close for the rest of their lives. In later years Maine would invite Sir James as his guest at the Christmas festivities at Trinity Hall where Maine was the Master. This was the background which led Sir James to appoint first Maine's son, and then his own son to the South Wales circuit.

It was not an appointment that impressed Stephen's uncle Leslie. He wrote 'Clearer symptoms showed themselves before long of the disease caused by the accident. I have no wish to dwell upon that painful topic...... it gradually became manifest that he was suffering from a terrible disease. He had painful periods of excitement and depression. Eccentricities of behaviour caused growing anxiety to his family'. Much more deserving was the appointment, also by Sir James of Stephen's brother Herbert to the clerkship of Assize to the Northern circuit the following year.

Sir James's last throw of the dice to save Stephen's legal career failed. Stephen delegated all the work to an assistant, and made no contribution himself. He did collect a small salary for nominally holding the position. It seemed his mind was too restless to hold down a job requiring discipline and thoroughness. In 1890 he resigned his clerkship of Assize, and the last chance of a life at the Bar was gone.

Chapter 11

The Shadow of Jack the Ripper

If Stephen's father believed matters could get no worse for his son who was now heading for two failed careers and personal instability, he was wrong. Stephen was on the edge of becoming embroiled in a series of killings, which became known as the Jack the Ripper case. It was and remains Britain's worst unsolved serial murder crime. Even Queen Victoria was moved to comment that 'every effort must be made to find the person responsible for these dreadful murders of unfortunate women of bad class'. Somehow Stephen became a suspect and a central figure in the case. He was questioned by the senior police officer leading the investigation, and was subsequently named as the culprit by several serious commentators.

The main source of this devastating speculation was an account which is supposed to have been given by the artist Walter Sickert to his son Joseph. He claimed that in 1884 when Stephen and Prince Edward were at Cambridge together, Stephen, who was something of a social secretary to the Prince's activities introduced him to a distant cousin Annie Crook. After a while the Prince and Annie Crook began an affair, which was not so surprising given the Prince's propensity for sexual activity in most forms. Sickert's story went on to record that after a while Annie became pregnant and on 18 April 1885 she gave birth to a daughter, Alice Margaret, at the Marylebone Workhouse. Alice's birth certificate still exists, but the father's name was left blank. By the mores of the day to fall pregnant outside marriage was a disgrace, and it would be usual for the man responsible to abandon the woman, perhaps with an allowance. The story, if true would have had to be kept from the public at all costs, as the population could not cope with the idea of a future monarch fathering an illegitimate child. So Stephen bore some responsibility for instigating this alleged scandal. At the time of the birth both he and the Prince were still at Cambridge. He would have known the consequences of his introduction.

At this stage it has to be said that recent genealogical research does not confirm the proposition that Stephen and Annie Crook were in any way related. There is a remote possibility that Annie's father William Crook was an illegitimate son of one of the Stephen family, and it may be from here that the story comes. Even if Stephen and Annie were not related it is still possible that Stephen made the introduction or at least was present when the two met. The venue for the supposed meeting would probably have been the Cleveland Club in Cleveland Street W1. This was a well known gay club for the wealthy and aristocratic, and it was later to be the subject of a sensational trial, before which several members including some peers (and the Prince) absented themselves from the country rather quickly. Stephen was not a member of the club, even his indulgent father would have baulked at paying a membership fee for such an establishment. However as a friend of the Prince, Stephen would have been welcome at anytime. All the evidence suggests that Stephen would have been interested in the services on offer, which often involved boys from the Telegraph Exchange opposite the club, who were working to supplement their modest incomes.

Another reason why the Prince and Annie Crook could have

met at the club was because she worked in a confectionery and tobacco shop down the street at No 22. Furthermore she lived a few doors down from the club at No 6. The address, 6 Cleveland Street is shown on Alice's birth certificate. The story, which has been pieced together from known facts, Walter Sickert's account, and subsequent investigations, now becomes even more dangerous to the Prince and, by association, Stephen. Annie Crook shared her home with a West End prostitute, Mary Kelly, who she employed as a nanny. Kelly worked in a club in the West End, and in view of her address, this was probably the Cleveland. Thus Kelly was aware of the background of Alice. In late 1886, 6 Cleveland Street was demolished, and Kelly moved to the East End to continue her trade in even less salubrious surroundings. It was now, according to conspiracy theorists, that matters got out of hand in terms of hushing up Alice's background. Kelly, a woman with alcoholic tendencies found it impossible not to gossip about the affair with some of her prostitute friends in local East End public houses, as a means of adding some colour to their sordid, poverty stricken lives. The cat was climbing out of the bag, and something drastic had to be done, and quickly. In an effort to suppress the rumours, and the gossip at least five prostitutes were murdered in the autumn of 1888 in the Whitechapel area. The last, in November, was Mary Kelly. They became known as the Jack the Ripper murders. This then was the essence of Sickert's story.

In early April 1888, it was evident that The Reflector was doomed. It had by then run to fourteen issues and Stephen realised its days were numbered. He was in despair, and was nowhere near stable enough to handle this setback with any equanimity. Less than three weeks before the paper folded on 21 April a call-girl named Emma Smith was attacked near the Whitechapel Road, and died the next day, 4 April, of her injuries.

It was because of this murder that the police opened the Whitechapel murders file. The file took in all those crimes attributed to Jack the Ripper, and it was not closed until both Stephen and the Prince were dead in 1892. Detective Constable Walter Dew, who was responsible for the Whitechapel area at the time, wrote in his autobiography 'I have always held that Emma Smith was the first to meet her death at the hands of Jack the Ripper'. Dew entered the history books of criminology when he tracked down and arrested the American murderer Dr Crippen in mid-Atlantic in 1909. Usually the Ripper murders are not thought to have begun until the end of August, but there is a case for believing that they began four months earlier. A very circumstantial case could be made that Stephen, upset by his literary failure, with a total commitment to the Prince and an awareness that he had set the ball rolling four years earlier, was involved. Moreover, an examination of his poetry does indicate evidence of an aversion to women. An example of this is in the verse:

'If all the harm that women have done,
Were put in a bundle and rolled into one,
Earth would not hold it,
The sky could not enfold it,
It could not be lighted nor warmed by the sun:
Such masses of evil
Would puzzle the devil
And keep him in fuel while Time's wheels run

But if all the harm that's been done by men
Were doubled and doubled and doubled again,
And melted and fused into vapour and then
Were squared and raised to the power of ten
There wouldn't be nearly enough, not near
To keep a small girl for the tenth of a year

This was all very unpleasant, but it was balanced, to some extent, by Stephen's rant against the man who trod on his foot during the train journey in Belgium.

There are other examples of Stephen's supposed misogyny. In another verse called In the Backs he writes:

> 'I should not like her: and I should not mind
> If she were done away with, killed or ploughed
> She did not seem to serve a useful end
> And certainly she was not beautiful'

Later on at Cambridge, Stephen founded the Walpole Society and proposed in its first debate 'that the female sex stands in need of repression'.

Sickert's story that Stephen's cousin, Annie Crook, bore the Prince a child does seem seriously flawed. The child was born on 18 April, which meant she was conceived mid-July the previous year. It is known that the Prince was at Heidelberg University from mid-June until the third week of August 1884. The baby could, of course, have been a month late or premature. Two other lesser points also reduce the likelihood of the Prince being the father. For the father's name to be missing from the birth certificate was normal in the case of illegitimacy, and it is hard to see how the Prince, in many ways a kindly man, would allow a child of his to be born in a workhouse. It is more likely that the Prince was not the only man with whom Annie Crook was conducting an affair.

In more recent years many authors have published theories to establish that Stephen at least had a hand in the murders. Frank Spiering, whose book was described by an American reviewer as 'concocted Grade Z fiction' suggested that Prince Edward had seen inside an East End slaughterhouse, and then, deranged by what he had witnessed, rushed into the night and hacked a prostitute to death. He picked on such women, so the tale goes, because he had become infected with syphilis as a result of a dalliance with such a lady. At least it is true that the Prince had syphilis when he died, and that he consorted with prostitutes. Stephen became implicated when the Prince admitted the murders to him. The story continues but the implausible deteriorates into the nonsensical.

Another book called Clarence written by Michael Harrison in 1972 points the finger more firmly at Stephen, but his reasoning is somewhat far fetched, and is backed by no hard facts at all. Briefly his theory rests on the suggestion that the Prince and Stephen had been lovers at Cambridge (which is possible) but once they had left the university they saw less of each other. Stephen felt abandoned, and realised that his influence had waned. He became even more upset when he realised that the Prince was visiting gay clubs without him and using prostitutes. Driven on by this jealousy, Stephen now increasingly wild, and tormented by the thought of the Prince with other men, and even women, set off on a series of mad revenge attacks.

A further book The Ripper and the Royals is based on Walter Sickert's story, which has already been outlined. It goes on to suggest that the murders were a team effort, which included Lord Randolph Churchill the organiser, Sir William Gull the actual murderer and some high ranking Freemasons who felt that the scandal threatened the future of the monarchy. Stephen, claimed Sickert, was one of a group of assistants, 'like a shooting party making a foray into the country'. At length Churchill decided that Annie Crook and Alice would have to be killed as well, but this was too much for Stephen. His regard for 'his' Prince was paramount, and he reported the whole sequence of events and murders to Detective Inspector Frederick Abbeline. This part of the story is to an extent supported by facts. On 15 December 1889, Abberline wrote to George Goschen, the Chancellor of the Exchequer who would have been able to authorise funds for the enterprise, saying:

> 'Sir,
>
> With respect to your last instruction my interviews with J K Stephen, Lord Randolph Churchill and Sir W Gull, were confirmed. I am sending this report for your personal attention. No further investigations will be made. I leave this in your hand. I have done my duty. Rest of my report will be sent on.
>
> Yours respectfully D I   F G Abberline'

This report never came to light. All the principal players were Freemasons – Abberline, Goschen, Churchill and probably Gull plus Abberline's superiors, Sir Charles Warren, the Commissioner of the Metropolitan Police and Sir Robert Anderson. The letter puts Stephen in amongst some of the most senior politicians and policemen in the land, and as a non-Freemason he was the odd man out.

In November 1970 a surgeon Mr Thomas Stowell claimed he had seen the private papers of Sir William Gull. These referred to a man named as 'S', and mentioned 'a distinguished family with titles'. Prince Edward was thought to be the man in question but the clues could equally well have fitted Stephen. Unfortunately Stowell's papers were never properly examined, and on his death shortly afterwards, his son destroyed them. Nevertheless Stowell's claims caused a sensation at the time, as it was the first occasion that the Prince's name had come to public attention as a serious suspect. In fact unknown to the population at the time, the Prince had been under police investigation. In 1889 the Metropolitan Police set up a top-secret inquiry at the Rochester Row police station in Westminster to decide if the Prince could possibly have been the culprit. Nothing became of it.

One person who did actually accuse Stephen of the murders was a Mrs Marny Hallam who wrote to the Sunday Times on 16 February 1975. In it, she said that her grandmother's father had been a barrister and that he had told her that the Ripper was 'one J K Stephen a tutor at Cambridge, one of whose students was the Duke of Clarence'. Andy Parlour a Ripperology researcher, tracked down Marny Hallam to talk to her about this claim, but by this time she was elderly and rather confused. Nevertheless Parlour managed to establish that some of Marny's forbears had worked at Lincoln's Inn as barristers in the 1880s, and had addresses close to Stephen's offices. Although the story has never had great credibility, it is intriguing that Stephen's name should be raised in this way nearly a hundred years after the event.

There are endless suspicions about who the murderer might have been, but it is curious that most of those that have reached publication give Stephen a role, sometimes a leading one. Apart from those mentioned, the American Dr David Abrahamsen believed that it was Stephen and the Prince acting together who were responsible and the author John Wilding claims that it was Stephen and his friend from Lincoln's Inn, Montague Druitt who committed the killings. The theory went that Druitt fell under the influence of Stephen at Lincoln's Inn, because of the latter's royal and aristocratic connections, his amusing eccentric manner, and his persuasively intelligent arguments.

Druitt came from a similar background to Stephen, but he

was a more solid character. His greatest joy was playing cricket. This he did very well at club level. He was a member of M C C, Blackheath, Incogniti, and the Butterflies, and as a cricketer he played with and against, some of the great names of the day. These included Lord Harris, Robert Abel, Ivo Bligh and Alfred Shaw. Druitt got to know Prince Edward partly through Stephen, and partly because the Prince was a frequent visitor to Lord Wimborne's estate where for ten years Druitt had been a welcome cricketer and guest. He therefore fitted in well with the Oxbridge milieu of the law courts and he soon discovered that he and Stephen had several mutual friends there.

Druitt has long been a leading suspect in his own right, although real evidence against him is non-existent. The whole case rests on some notes put together by Sir Melville Macnaghten, the Commissioner of the Metropolitan Police five years after Druitt's death. The notes are now realised to be valueless and were written to divert attention away from a police colleague who had been identified by the Sun newspaper as the murderer. As a dead non-Freemason, Druitt fitted the role of scapegoat admirably. His only 'mistake' was to be found drowned in late December 1888, six weeks after the last Ripper murder, in the Thames at Chiswick, immediately outside Harry Wilson's Osiers chummery. Druitt's presence in the vicinity of the Osiers does support the view that, if not a member, he was a least a visitor and his friendship with so many habitués would have gained him entrance. The nature of the club may also be relevant. Druitt had been fired from his position at the boy's school just before his death, for an unspecified offence, and the feeling was that he had sought refuge at The Osiers, where he could expect help and advice. Druitt's inquest, which was quickly and sketchily carried out, returned a verdict of suicide by drowning. Yet there is a good case for wondering if more senior members of the club saw Druitt in a fragile state, and feared he would reveal too much of the antics of the Prince, Harry Wilson and sundry other well known personages. Whatever the precise circumstances of his death, it is most unlikely that Druitt had anything to do with the murders. His supposed alliance with Stephen was merely a convenient way of putting together two suspects, who were friends and who could be linked by a notional homosexuality. In no respect did Druitt fit the profile of a murderer. He had no medical experience, a DNA assessment commissioned by Patricia Cornwell, the American crime writer, found no link, and the processes of psychological and 'Geographic' profiling, all put Druitt in the clear. Furthermore the dates and venues of cricket matches in which Druitt played, make it very improbable for him to have been at the scenes of the earlier murders. At the time of the killings there is every indication that his life as a schoolmaster, barrister, and director of Blackheath Cricket Club was progressing normally and enjoyably.

Nor can the Prince be regarded as a remotely plausible suspect. The five acknowledged Ripper murders occurred between 31 August and 9 November 1888, which included two on 30 September. The court and royal records show the Prince to have been staying in Yorkshire with Viscount Downe at the time of the first murder and at the Cavalry Barracks in York for the second. At the time of the 'Double Event' murder he was lunching with his grandmother at Abergeldie in Scotland, and for the fifth he was at Sandringham. If he had ever needed an alibi, his was cast iron, and it was the reason why the Metropolitan police soon gave up their inquiry.

Stephen's role, if any, in the Whitechapel case is made more complicated by so many different theories. The Abberline letter to George Goschen does support the view that Stephen was somehow involved, and if the conspiracy theory to protect the reputation of Prince Edward has any truth then Stephen's part becomes more likely. Even if Stephen knew about the plot and even supported it for the sake of his friend, it is a long way from declaring him the murderer. If the idea of a conspiracy is a fabrication then the likelihood of Stephen's involvement declines sharply. There is no direct evidence against Stephen. More specifically, he did not have the medical knowledge to eviscerate the women in the skilled way that was done. Nearly all the doctors, police surgeons, and post mortem reports refer to the necessity for the killer to have had professional medical knowledge. It is difficult to completely ignore so many theories that involve Stephen, but the worst that can be said of him is that he probably knew something about the matter if the protection of the Prince and the Royal Family was the objective.

Whatever the truth, the scandal has swamped Stephen's reputation for over 100 years and instead of being remembered as a 'Master of Light Verse' as he was described in the Times Literary Supplement on the 50th anniversary of his death, he is dismissed as yet another Jack the Ripper suspect. Stephen may have been odd at times, even unbalanced, but he surely does not deserve the description as 'the worst Britain in the last 1000 years'. This was the title 'won' by Jack the Ripper in a poll of 5000 people conducted by the BBC, and published in 2006.

Chapter 12

Family Affairs

Setting aside the matter of the murders, Stephen spent the second half of 1888 still endeavouring to restore his literary reputation. He did so with a series of articles for the Pall Mall Gazette, the St James's Gazette and the Etonian. His new position of clerk to South Wales Assizes was an irrelevance to him and he seemed singularly ungrateful for the efforts his father was making on his behalf. He continued to live at De Vere Gardens. It is probable that he spent much time at that scholarly refuge, the Savile Club. This would have been important to him as a way of escaping into a more cultured world, as he saw it. In the October he supported the membership application of Oscar Wilde to the Club, which in fact the committee never approved. Other prospective members who Stephen put forward were Gerald Duckworth, the half brother of Virginia Woolf, Arthur Hort and James Duncan. They all subsequently merited entries in Who's Who, and Charles Connan was featured in the Directory of National Biography. Names such as these suggest the sort of circles in which Stephen liked to move.

If 1888 had been a bad year for Stephen, 1889 was to prove an even worse one for his father. Sir James had risen to the rank of High Court Judge on the Queen's Bench largely through his competent work in India. He had little in the way of real court experience, and no political background. The first signs that all was not well with Sir James occurred in 1885 when he had what was described by his son James, as 'a serious illness'. He appeared to have recovered until he presided over a trial in July 1887 concerning a man called Israel Lipski. Briefly, at the end of June, a woman named Miriam Angel was murdered in the East End, and Lipski was accused of doing it by pouring acid down her throat. His defence was not believed by the jury and Sir James sentenced him to death. However in his summing up the judge suggested that Lipski's motive was lust, but this had never been put forward by the prosecution, so the defence had no chance or need to refute it. Such was the public outcry against the verdict and the sentence, led by the Pall Mall Gazette, that the Home Secretary, Henry Matthews, and Sir James met for a series of desperate last minute meetings to work out the basis for a reprieve. Suddenly as if by magic, a confession from Lipski was brought in, and he was hanged a few hours later. Few believed that justice had been done, and one paper reminded its readers 'it is well to remember that the witches who were burnt in the seventeenth century almost always confessed their guilt, or were said to have done so'. W T Stead, the editor of the Pall Mall Gazette referred to Sir James as Mr 'Injustice' Stephen. However Sir James's career survived but his reputation was questioned.

The final damage occurred when Sir James was taking a case, in some ways similar, two years later. A Florence Maybrick from Liverpool was accused of poisoning her husband, James, but despite a well conducted and convincing defence, led by Sir Charles Russell, Sir James seemed determined that the jury return a guilty verdict. His summing up was seen by the judiciary, and public, as biased. He told the jury that Mrs Maybrick had committed adultery, although no evidence had been presented in court to support this, and that adulteresses were more likely to commit murder. Sir James duly got his guilty verdict, and sentenced Mrs Maybrick to death. This time however the outcry was too much. He was attacked in the press and received abusive mail. Accusations were made that he was jealous of the defence team, and of misogyny. Sir James was on record as saying he disliked ladies attending trials, which he felt encouraged promiscuity. Once he caused offence by using the term 'women' in a demeaning manner rather than the appropriate 'ladies'. As a result the Home Secretary, still Henry Matthews, ordered the sentence to be commuted to life imprisonment. Florence Maybrick served fifteen years. Charles Russell was not satisfied, and issued a litany of alleged misdirections that Sir James had carried out. Russell later became Lord Chief Justice of England. There was one strange twist to the story. In 1992 a diary which it was claimed belonged to Mrs Maybrick's husband, was found in Liverpool. In it James Maybrick admits responsibility for the Ripper murders. This caused great interest, and there are today some students of the murders who believe it is genuine. The balance of opinion, though, is that it is not.

This last gaffe by Sir James was too much even for a tolerant, protective judiciary, and it was to prove his last trial. In 1900 the Liverpool Daily Post was still campaigning for the release of Mrs Maybrick. It described Sir James as a 'great mad judge'. It went on:

'Nothing more painful was ever seen in court than the proud old man's desperate struggle to control his failing faculties. But the struggle was unavailing. It was clear that the growing volume of facts was unassorted, undigested in his mind; that his judgement swayed backward and forward in the conflict of testimony; that his memory failed to grip the most salient features of the case for many minutes together. It was shocking to think that a human life depended upon the direction of this wreck of what was once a great judge'.

No word of reply or complaint was heard from the Stephen family. Ironically, The Post was protected from prosecution by a landmark judgment that Sir James himself had made that 'the dead cannot be libelled'. A more measured verdict of Sir James's time on the Bench appeared in the Directory of National Biography. It said:

'Stephen's thirteen years on the Bench were unimpressive when put alongside his intellectual vigour and achievements in other fields. Stephen's failure as a judge was relative rather than absolute. As a judge he produced a very respectable collection of criminal first instances and appeal judgements. Yet when measured against a broader span of significant instances of judicial creativity beyond criminal law, none of Stephen's contributions could be regarded as of fundamental conceptual importance'.

In truth he was a limited conservative judge whose view of reform was summed up in his own words 'Progress has its drawbacks, and they are great and serious'.

Sir James's difficulties, politely referred to at the time as 'overwork', were more likely due to a gradual mental breakdown. The Stephen family was particularly unfortunate in this respect. By the time of the Maybrick trial, James Stephen had been showing increasing signs of imbalance. On his uncle's side, the record became steadily worse. Leslie Stephen himself had a record of depression and suffered three nervous breakdowns; his son Thoby threatened to kill himself as a schoolboy, and his daughter by his first marriage, Laura, did go insane in her twenties. Most notable of all was the death by suicide of Virginia Woolf, yet another of Stephen's cousins, in 1941. This followed countless breakdowns and suicide threats. Even her husband Leonard Woolf contemplated suicide when Britain was under threat from Germany in the Second World War.

The manner of Virginia Woolf's death brought up more echoes of the Ripper story. By weighting her overcoat with heavy stones and stepping into the River Ouse at Rodmell in Sussex, she replicated the way Stephen's old friend Montague Druitt was alleged to have drowned in the Thames. She would have known the story of Druitt and how he died from her cousin James, or her uncle Sir James, both of whom knew Druitt, and would have been interested in his possible involvement in the Whitechapel murders. It was a tale that would have gone into family folklore, and fifty years later Virginia Woolf remembered it.

There were others in the Stephen clan whose behaviour was not normal. Gerald Duckworth, a publisher, who Stephen was to propose for the Savile Club, made an indecent advance to a very young Virginia Woolf. In her words 'I still shiver with shame at the memory of my half-brother standing me on a ledge, aged about 6, and exploring my private parts'. The incident affected Woolf for the rest of her life. It may have contributed to her taking female lovers, amongst them Madge Vaughan, daughter of John Symonds who was another relative by marriage to Stephen, and Vita Sackville-West.

It was the Stephen family that formed the nucleus of the Bloomsbury Set, a movement that emerged at Cambridge. There it was known as the Midnight Society, and met on Saturdays at midnight to read poetry and plays. It started at the end of the 19th century. The participants appeared to be an impossibly narcissistic group of undergraduates trying too hard to be seen as emergent intellectuals. Amongst their number who went on to form the Bloomsbury circle were Clive Bell, Lytton Strachey and Leonard Woolf, who was to marry Virginia. Bell was the art critic who adopted the phrase 'significant form', and took the rather arrogant view that the mass of the population could not make an aesthetic judgment. Strachey was a biographer whose book 'Eminent Victorians' caused literary uproar when it challenged the smug self-assurance of the Victorian era. Woolf wrote several books on social and political matters, and founded the Hogarth Press.

Once the Bloomsbury Set evolved in 1904, their ranks were joined by many of the leading talents such as Vanessa and Virginia Stephen (as they were), Duncan Grant, Roger Fry and J M Keynes. Vanessa Stephen was a life-time artist who formed the Friday Club to encourage amateur and professional painters. Virginia scarcely needs an introduction. She was one of the most celebrated novelists of the 20th century. Her works included 'To the Lighthouse', 'The Voyage Out', and 'Orlando'. Grant was a painter, somewhat in the style of Cezanne, and his work has endured. Fry's painting was similarly influenced. In addition he was a respected art critic and expounded a theory of 'aesthetic philosophy'. John Keynes was the economist of the group. A graduate of Eton and King's Cambridge, he became a government advisor on economics during the First World War, but sometimes his theories became too controversial for general acceptance. The group met in Brunswick and Gordon Squares in the Bloomsbury area of London, but they were not considered particularly significant, until years after their disbandment. Then the name was taken up by people wishing to exploit its reputation and for a while it became a most fashionable group to belong to. It was a rather amorphous collection of creative and philosophical dogma. It embraced writers, artists, poets and art critics. Its credo was to regard normal worldly values as stupid; it rejected wealth and the trappings of success and invented a philosophy of 'ethical evolution'. It veered between the very frivolous and the very serious. Part of the attraction to its members was that it was considered exclusive. Its legacy is to be remembered as a collection of slightly weird, bright people most of whom had enough talent to be significant in their own right, and did not need the doubtful prestige of forming a group. It is debatable if Bloomsbury had a lasting value. Not everyone was, or has been, impressed. John Carey reviewing a biography of Leonard Woolf in the Sunday Times in 2006 described the group as 'an absurd bunch, bloated with self-esteem'. He quoted Lytton Strachey's proclamation 'we are the mysterious priests of a new and amazing civilisation'.

Most of the Society's leading members were Apostles. This included Strachey, Woolf, Keynes and Fry. Women were not admitted to the Apostles and Virginia Woolf's view was disapproving. She believed 'they were clever and unworldly, but arrogant, prickly and withdrawn. They were men who tended to be devoid of female company'. It was a more thoughtful, perceptive opinion than most at the time. As the two groups, the Apostles and Bloomsbury had so many mutual members, this was an indirect criticism of the latter of which she was a leading member. The commonality of membership was not surprising since there were distinct similarities between the Apostles and Bloomsbury. Both had no clear cut ideas about politics, art or literature, both could embrace contrasting ideas if they were sincerely held, both doubted the pedestal status of the family, and both could tolerate the serious and the trivial.

At the end of 1889 Stephen's health was not good, and a family friend and physician Dr George Savage was asked to help. He was another of Leslie Stephen's 'Sunday Tramps' colleagues. Savage's credentials were excellent. He had trained at Guy's Hospital and was qualified in neurology, mental physiology, and most aspects of brain disorders. His most famous client was Virginia Woolf who he treated from 1904, but he was known to her long before then, and had talked to her about Stephen's condition. She told the story of how Stephen would ride around London for hours in a hansom cab, then rush into her house, and demand the driver be paid. Another time Stephen decided to take up painting and insisted that Virginia and her mother should accompany him to De Vere Gardens. There Virginia posed for him, and he painted her on a piece of wood. She was eight years old. After one session with Dr Savage, Stephen told Virginia with some glee that 'Savage has just told me I'm in danger of dying or going mad'. Leslie Stephen reported in the middle of 1890 'We are uncomfortable about Jem. He lies in bed all morning, and seems unable to rouse himself to anything. I got him to come and play billiards on Saturday. I then proposed a walk on Sunday, but when the time came he could not be roused to come out. It is very sad'. The 'walk on Sunday' was probably a 'Sunday Tramp' of which Stephen, at least nominally, was a member.

While Stephen was going into decline, his great friend and pupil, Prince Edward was having his own difficulties. The scandalous Cleveland Street trial was coming to an end. It had involved politicians, bankers and members of the aristocracy participating in a male brothel of the same name. Prince Edward had been a member. He was referred to in the Department of Public Prosecutions file of patrons as P.A.V. (Prince Albert Victor). He also belonged to a club round the corner called the Hundred Guineas. There, as was the custom, the Prince had to use a female nickname. His was Victoria. It was a club with few restrictions, for example after 2 .00 am the staff were instructed to oblige customers with any service required.

The essence of the Cleveland Street scandal was that boys from the Telephone Exchange opposite the club of the same name could supplement their wages by 'obliging' society members. The normal fee was £1, of which the boy received 4/- (20p). The balance went to the club's owner, Charles Hammond. For a long time the police were under instructions to turn a blind eye to proceedings, due to the influence of club members, which even reached into the judiciary. Eventually the club's activities became too notorious and flagrant, and the Director of Public Prosecutions had to act. It was at this point, with a court case looming, that Hammond and several of the main participants including Lord Arthur Somerset, the manager of the royal stables, and equerry to Prince Edward's father, were spirited abroad. It was essential too that Prince Edward was moved well away from the trial, so a tour of India was conveniently arranged for him. He did not return to England until well after the trial was over in the spring of 1890. The ring leader at the Post Office, George Veck received a very lenient four months in prison, and several of the boys were sent to Australia with £20, a pound a week for three years, and a new suit as compensation. The main culprits escaped.

Edward's name had been successfully kept out of the newspapers during the trial, but his parents and grandmother did understand the reality of the matter. It was from this moment they decided that he could not be King. Their solution was to give Edward a new title, which might sound to the unwary that he had been promoted. In fact it was a demotion with all sorts of unfortunate historical connotations. On 24

May it was announced that Edward was to be known as the Duke of Clarence and Avondale and Earl of Athlone. Although this may have sounded impressive the fact was the Edward had slipped from being a Prince to a Duke. It was a none too subtle message that he would never ascend to the throne. The choice of the 'Duke of Clarence' part of the title was particularly unkind. The only well known holder of that title had been drowned in a vat of malmsey wine in the Tower of London in 1478. His crime had been to plot the overthrow of his brother Edward IV. The only other Duke of Clarence of note was the third son of George III, and he did become king as Willian IV in 1830. However he blotted his copybook by not producing a legitimate heir. He had twelve children, but only two in wedlock and as these died in infancy the crown had to be passed to his niece, Victoria. It was not an appointment with an enviable reputation.

Chapter 13

Warnings and Rejections

The last three months of 1890 were a catalogue of setbacks and frustrations for Stephen. It was a time when his lack of judgment at last caught up with him. In October he resigned the clerkship of South Wales and finally said goodbye to any prospect of a legal career. His father was less than pleased, and it led to Stephen moving out of De Vere Gardens, and briefly renting rooms in Half Moon Street, off Piccadilly. His plan was that he would take a holiday and then return to Cambridge to teach or tutor in law and history. His old friend Oscar Browning was still very much part of the scene, and he expected to be able to find some paid employment.

At the end of the same month George Savage who had been monitoring Stephen's mental condition since 1888, became aware of the deterioration. Savage knew from talks with Leslie Stephen something of the Stephen family background including Sir James's breakdown in 1885. Savage now expressed the opinion that Stephen 'was not in a state of perfect mental health' and was suffering from 'morbid excitement or cerebral exaltation'. He advised that Stephen ought to be put under restraint, or at least be sent to a quiet, distant place for several months, preferably under the close supervision of a doctor. He believed it would be unwise for Stephen to travel to London, Cambridge or Paris. Stephen rejected this out of hand and made a point of visiting each of these places in the next few weeks.

However, Savage had reached his conclusion without examining or even interviewing Stephen. This had been done by Sir Andrew Clark, Dr Hughlings Jackson, and Dr Hack Tuke. These men were all eminent specialists in diagnosing and treating disorders of the brain. All reported that Stephen was normal. Clark said he was 'in perfect physical condition'; Jackson reported the same about his nervous system, and Tuke could find no trace of brain disease. On what Savage based his recommendations, is a mystery. Nevertheless on 21 November, Savage wrote the following letter which was sealed up and marked 'not to be opened until May 1891'

On 1 May Stephen opened the letter, it read:

'3, Henrietta Street
Cavendish Square W
November 21 1890

Dear Stephen

According to promise I write my opinion as to the next 6 months of your life. For some weeks to come there will be a waste of money, buying useless things, ie things for which you have no real need. You will borrow money right and left. You will dress in unconventional ways and cause worry to your relations. You will discover that you have incurred debts which of yourself you cannot pay and will feel it a grievance that you have to fall in with the conditions which are imposed. You will then take to bed and spend much of the spring in reading in bed and doing nothing of any good, not earning a living. The period will be one rather of exhaustion than of depression, and so the circle will be completed.

I am, Yours truly G H Savage'

As it turned out this was quite an accurate prophecy of how Stephen would behave over the six months after his legal career had ended.

Stephen was furious and wrote a long pamphlet condemning Savage's forecast. He argued that nothing Savage had predicted had come true, and that he was leading a responsible life. The full text of Stephen's pamphlet is shown in the Appendices.

Savage's assessment of Stephen was accepted because of his seniority, reputation and his long standing relationship with the Stephen family, but he was not infallible. Years later after treating Virginia Woolf he declared her fully recovered and capable of leading a normal life in London. Within a few months, she had had a breakdown and the trust between the doctor and the family ended. There was one final piece of the jigsaw that impacted on Savage's relationship with the Stephen family, and it had a direct connection with the Ripper case. In the Fortnightly Review of the Illustrated Police News dated 6 October 1888, Savage wrote an article under the headline 'Homicidal Mania'. He described this term as having no medical validity since 'there is no form of medical disease which has as its only characteristic a thirst for blood'. He believed that murderous tendencies could be traced back to instances of cruelty in childhood towards insects or animals, and that epilepsy was often an origin of these impulses. Savage claimed that the more purposeless the crime, the more this was likely to be true. Savage's piece was written before the two murders on 30 September, but because of these killings, it took on a special significance when it was published. It was widely seen as a commentary on the Whitechapel murders. In the same edition of the Police News there were long detailed accounts of both murders and the inquests, adding to the relevancy of Savage's views. It can only be a coincidence that the autumn of 1888 was when Savage became Stephen's main health advisor.

It was also in late 1890 that a calamity befell Stephen, which in its way was almost as devastating as the failure of The Reflector two years earlier. He was expelled from the Savile Club. In the November and December the Savile Committee met five times to consider Stephen's behaviour. His misdemeanours were sadly familiar. Firstly he was refusing to pay his bills, and secondly he was showing violence to other members and to the staff. The committee was reluctant to take the ultimate step. Stephen had been a member for ten years and 'a model Savilian'. Further, he had had respected proposers and supporters when he joined and he had put up for membership some valued new members. Leslie Stephen, also a long standing member, tried to defend him on the grounds he had a mental illness brought on by the Felixstowe accident. However, Stephen had become such a nuisance that the committee had to expel him – an event rare in the Club's history. As a consequence Stephen was banned from the club's premises. He reacted so violently that extra staff had to be engaged and the police called to prevent him getting back into the club. In January 1891 he wrote a angry letter to the committee, as follows:

'The following letter has been addressed to the Committee of the Savile Club

King's College,
Cambridge,
Jan. 29th, 1891

Gentlemen,

    I find that it will be necessary to write you one more letter, of which a copy will be sent to every member of the Club. For reasons with which I have acquainted you in detail, I hold that your conduct towards me has been mean, treacherous and disingenuous, as well as tyrannical, narrow-minded and brutal. You have behaved in a way, which proves you to be unworthy to occupy any position of trust, or to represent, for any purpose, any body of English Gentlemen. I cannot discern in your behaviour one trait of good-feeling, one spark of generosity, or any indication whatever of an acquaintance with the ways of gentlemen or of men of the world. If any of you choose at once personally to dissociate yourselves from the action of the majority, I will consider the possibility of remaining on terms of friendship or acquaintance with them. With no one of the others will I ever hold any communications, written or verbal.

I have the honour to be,
Gentlemen,
Your faithful servant,
J K STEPHEN.'

His expulsion was a disgrace on the carefully honed name of the Stephen family and the matter rankled. So much so that over thirty years later, the Committee, possibly urged on by Stephen's brother Herbert, who was by now a very senior member, ordered through the secretary Geoffrey Williams, that all correspondence relating to the decision should be destroyed. Further, wherever Stephen's name was referred to in the meetings of the November and December, it should be cut out of the records and minutes. Williams did a thorough job, and to this day the relevant pages of the books show a number of 'windows'. The other person who may have influenced this censorship was Gerald Duckworth, who having been proposed by Stephen remained a member until his death in 1937. For a time, he was the Club's secretary.

At the same time that Stephen's career at the Savile Club was coming to an end, he began to be troublesome in another, unlikely, direction. He decided he was in love with Stella Duckworth.   It was a wild, sometimes violent pursuit. Leslie Stephen wanted to ban him from the house at Hyde Park Gate, but his wife Julia, Stephen's aunt, would not allow it 'I cannot shut my door upon Jem' she said. She alone seemed capable of keeping Stephen under control and treated him like a son. She would visit his grave on the anniversaries of his death. Unfortunately 3 February 1895 was a particularly cold day and Julia caught influenza on the way to the cemetery. She died a month later. Leslie Stephen's children, though, were told to tell Stephen when he called, that Stella was away visiting relations or staying with the Lushingtons at Pyports. Often the family would leave by the back door to avoid bumping into Stephen, who might be loitering outside. Stephen was no better than a Victorian stalker. For her part Stella made it clear that these advances were entirely unwelcome. She was much more interested in helping her friend Octavia Hill with her charitable work amongst the homeless in Southwark.

Frustrated in his attempts to see Stella, Stephen started a flurry of correspondence, some of which still survives. His letter written on Savile Club paper on 25 October was full of gratuitous, philosophical advice about love, and relationships. The most interesting piece was Stephen's admission that 'I have had a good many intimate and confidential friendships with men and women'. The letter runs:

'Oct 25 90

One letter more, my Star, and I fear a long one and then I will drop the role of a sentimental lover and resume one I am much more fitted to play that of an affectionate cousin.

I am going to write to you exactly as if the gentleman who wanted to marry you was Tom, Dick or Harry, and as if you had asked for my advice. You would not be likely to do this but you might do. I am now getting middle aged and I know something of the world. I am an inquisitive man with a retentive memory. I have had a good many intimate and confidential friendships with men and women. I have known the curse of scorn. All these things give the man the capacity for admiring a girl and the fact that I am very fond of you Stella (quite independently of being in love) gives me a reason to use it. And first I would say. Do not marry any man unless your heart tells you quite unmistakenly that you love him. And if your heart does tell you so, be slow to believe it, and test the feeling in every way. Do not marry him until his presence is an hourly need, his opinion a necessity. His goodwill your greatest object, his love the highest joy you can conceive. Wait for love: it will come in time that he may love you too and that all will go well. Do not expect to find a man worthy of your love. I do not say this to flatter you Stella. No man can really be worthy of any good woman's love. Nor any woman of a good man's. You are not worthy of mine. Love is power or feeling in the human mind, springing I know not whence, which clothes its objects with such attributes as no human being ever possessed, or will possess. You for instance have no doubt your faults, though not many. In beauty, in goodness, in wisdom for me you realise perfection. That is because I love you and some day you will find a man, not less faulty than myself perhaps,, who will love you. For you he will be perfect and may your love for him go with you to the grave. You may come to love a man whom you have known and never thought to love. One by one all the things you like him for will become more and more numerous, until some small item of liking will be added and transmute the whole to love in a moment. This may happen to you as it happened to many. This is not much of a letter dear, but it is the best I can write. And so goodbye my Star, goodbye perhaps for ever.

Your affectionate cousin. Jem

Don't be sentimental: don't be excitable, don't be unsympathetic, don't above all be unreasonable so as to think I did wrong when you know I did right. Don't repeat the mistake, but be your own calm, quiet, sweet sober self'.

On the same day, perhaps in the morning Stephen wrote to Stella from De Vere Gardens. Again his thwarted, unreturned love is painfully clear. Part of the letter reads:

'Dear Stella,

'I was quite prepared for you saying nothing yesterday as I told you. Still I do want at your convenience an answer to this question. Do you believe I honestly and truly meant every word I said to you about my own feelings and about your conduct? I love you better than anything in the world, I have done these many months past

Ever your most loving JKS'

A week later, this time from King's College, Stephen again bares his soul, over his financial difficulties. He starts with the promise of turning over a new leaf:

'With you to back me up, I can defy the world. In the last three weeks I have saved nearly £20. I have £500 a year. Last year being ill I spent no money. I owe nothing that I cannot pay tomorrow. I have a balance in the bank, which I shall keep.

I have ruined my life. All this is true Stella on my word of honour. Love me a little Stella, my sweet silent Star. Jem'

The last of the surviving letters was also written from King's, this time on 11 November:

'Goodnight my darling. Do try to be kind truthful and (for the first and last time) obedient to your affection cousin, judicious councillor and true lover. Jem

I do so love you my Star. I shall not go to bed tonight, but you will. Dream happy, wake happy and bide your time. Sooner or later you will fall in love, be loved in return, marry and live happily ever after. Happy man! He will be worthy of you Stella. Jem'

There are no signs either in Stephen's letters or from other correspondence that Stephen ever received a reply. Stella's response or lack of it, was the antithesis of the American Maud du Puy's belief that 'the English girls are so awfully suspectible; if a man speaks to them almost, they instantly think he is desperately in love with them'. Stephen had the role of the rebuffed suitor, and it was a role he had never been used to. Within a few days his expulsion from the Savile Club was under way, and he was to find himself again rejected. He was spinning out of control.

Stephen was not the only one of his Cambridge friends who had difficulty in coping with the move towards heterosexuality. The elegantly named James Duff Duff, another classicist and Apostle, became engaged to Laura Lenox-Conyngham. He was descended from the Duffs of Hatton Castle and Knockleith in Aberdeenshire, and she was from a long established Ulster family. However, immediately after their betrothal, he suffered a nervous breakdown. His doctor was none other than George Savage who diagnosed 'fits of depression with profound despondency'. Duff was a member of Stephen's 'intellectual aristocracy', and a great career was predicted. Duff took the advice of Savage to break off the engagement. However Duff's latent love for Laura would not go away, and four years later he proposed again. This time the marriage went through and was a splendid success. They had five children and Duff's career at Trinity College was most effectively resurrected. Stephen was not so lucky.

Harry Cust had no such difficulty in making the transition, and built up a formidable and justified reputation amongst the aristocracy. The Marchioness of Londonderry and the Duchess of Rutland were but two of his conquests.

Chapter 14

An Incident in Paris

While Stephen was indulging in what could be termed 'inappropriate behaviour', the new Duke of Clarence, seemed to be doing his best to keep pace with him. For some time the Duke had been resorting to prostitutes, but this foible moved into a higher gear when he started writing letters to two of them. His action was unbelievably indiscreet and naïve. Eventually he realised the letters ought to be retrieved so he asked his solicitor George Lewis to handle the matter. Lewis made a good living by sorting out the social misjudgements of wealthy clients, including the Royal Family, in a way that would attract no public attention. For these services he was knighted in 1892.

On 17 November 1890 the Duke wrote to Lewis from Castle Rising near King's Lynn as follows:

'Dear Mr Lewis,

I hope you will forgive me for not having answered your letter before which I received on Sunday at Windsor, but I really have not had a moment to myself these last three days or you may be sure I would have written sooner. I am very pleased to hear you were able to settle with Miss Richardson although £200 is rather expensive for letters, but still I presume there is no other way of getting them back without paying that sum which I will be sending to you in a cheque. I heard from her two days ago saying she was very pleased to hear I was going to give her 200 and asked for another hundred, but as you have settled for the amount mentioned I hope the other will not be necessary for it does seem a strong idea to want more. But I can well understand her intention to get as much out of us as she can. I am very much obliged indeed to you for having settled matters so well, and I must be careful not to see her again. I suppose there is no doubt as to getting all the letters back for it might be awkward if she kept one or two back. I will also do all I can to get back one or two letters written to the other lady, and if unsuccessful will ask your assistance in the matter. But I think it can be managed with diplomacy.

Believe me, yours sincerely

Edward'

Two months later the situation was still worrying the Duke, so again he called in George Lewis. His personal note paper was headed Cavalry Barracks 15 January 1891:

'Dear Mr Lewis,

I hope you will accept from me a small gift in the shape of a fiver in acknowledgement for the kindness you showed me the other day in getting me out of that trouble that I was foolish enough to get into. I am anxious about the other lady when you last wrote to me, but I am glad to say that I think that little difficulty ought to be easily got over. I saw my friend a short time ago who said he would go and see the lady whom he knows well, and ask her to give up the other three letters I had written to her. But failing that to go and see you about it. After what I told him, he really thinks he will have no difficulty in getting them from her. You may be certain that I shall be careful in the future and not get into more trouble of this sort. If you have Miss R's letters, or rather mine and have not destroyed them, I should like to see them.

Believe me, yours sincerely   Edward'

The episode vindicates once again the conclusion of his family that he would be hopeless as a king, and their decision to reduce his rank to a Dukedom.

The two letters were auctioned at Bonham's in London in March 2002 and sold for over £8,000. The price in today's values was remarkably similar to the amount handed over for the incriminating royal letters over 100 years earlier. The buyer was anonymous but whoever sold these letters may have been fortunate to be rid of them. In the 1880s Charles Augustus Howell, a Victorian blackmailer came across two notes that Prince Edward had written to another cadet during his training spell on HMS Britannia. Howell's talent lay in securing evidence of scandal and pornography, and using it to his maximum advantage. However, in the spring of 1890 Howell was found in the gutter outside a Chelsea public house. His throat had been cut and a half sovereign had been wedged between his teeth – a traditional vengeance on a blackmailer. He died a few days later on 24 April at the Home Hospital, Fitzroy Square.

It was early in 1891 between ending his legal career and moving back to Cambridge that Stephen decided he would be a great artist. He felt that this complemented his literary work. He painted some watercolours, which he claimed were portraits and he showed them to Arthur Benson for approval. Benson described them as 'grotesque'. One in particular was of a female figure in a long brown coat sitting on a stile, on a moonlit night. To Benson 'it would seem though the female figure might be half-woman, half man'. There are also records of three other watercolours that Stephen attempted in the first two weeks of September 1891. He called them 'In a Garden', 'Autumn Thoughts', and 'After Sunset'. The only works to survive are at King's College, Cambridge, which has two postcard size caricatures. One shows Stephen cheering up a patient in a hospital bed, and the second features Oscar Browning in a similar bedside situation, but this time the patient looked close to death. Together they form a pair and because Stephen and Browning are so recognisable it does seem Stephen had rather more artistic talent than he was given credit for. He also attempted a few portraits of a very young Virginia Woolf.

It was also in 1891 that Stephen took it into his head to have his portrait painted. Possibly he wished to emulate his father for whom G F Watts had produced a chalk drawing portrait in 1855. This still hangs in the National Portrait Gallery. At any rate a very competent work featuring Stephen appeared at that time. It was by Charles Wellington Furse, a talented Victorian artist, who took his inspiration from the American James Whistler. He was a member of the Chelsea Arts Club, and the Royal Society of British Artists, and examples of his work can be found in the Grosvenor Gallery, and the Walker Art Gallery in Liverpool. There is a strange story connected with this picture which King's College found on a Cambridge website, but for which details are very sketchy. Apparently in 1977 the painting was vandalised, perhaps slashed with a knife. It was repaired and remains in position today. The local paper carried no reports of the incident and the police were not called. One long standing Cambridge resident has a hazy recollection, but the complete story remains at large. Furse was aged 23 when he painted Stephen, and it was through this assignment that Furse met the rest of the Stephen family including a childhood friend of Virginia Woolf called Katherine. It was this introduction that led to the marriage of Furse and Katherine. At the wedding Vanessa, Virginia's older sister, was a bridesmaid and Furse painted her portrait as well. He was rapidly building himself a reputation as a society portrait artist with a 'bold, voluptuous' style, but this promise could never be fully realised as he died aged 36 of tuberculosis. Had he lived he would have been a natural candidate to join the Bloomsbury Set.

The picture of Stephen, which hangs in the Combination Room in King's College, Cambridge, shows him in a carefully presented pose, wearing a red flower in his buttonhole as a characteristic touch of flamboyance. There was some speculation that the flower was an obscure message of support for the Freemasons' Knights Templars, although Stephen was never a member of that society. There are two other paintings done by Furse which related to Stephen's period at Eton and Cambridge. One was of the Bursar and Vice Provost of King's, Fred Whitting, whose picture hangs at King's, and the other is of an Eton housemaster named Henry Luxmoore. Luxmoore was a friend of Oscar Browning and Francis Cornish, Stephen's two main tutors. It is possible that this is where Stephen got the idea to commission Furse. Another portrait of Stephen was done by a less well-known artist named Frederick Miller in 1887, and is a head and shoulders chalk drawing. Stephen liked it so much he included it in the first edition of his book of verse, Lapsus Calami, which he published in 1891. Stephen's flirtation with painting was reported in The Academy in August 1905.

'He was keenly interested in painting, the sister art of poetry' as he claimed it to be in his verse 'Paint and Ink'. The poem was dedicated to Charles Wellington Furse, who painted his portrait, and whose talent Stephen greatly admired. In the poem he compared Furse's skills with his own writings:

'You take a brush, and I take a pen
You mix bright colours, I use black pen
You cover a canvas, you first of men
I write on a sheet for a scribbler meet.
Well, a contrast's a contrast. I will not shrink'

In his enthusiasm he took to carrying a pocket paint box, and attempted a few more watercolours but his ambition was never likely to be realised. There seems little support for the view that Stephen had much artistic talent, and the exercise proved to be a passing fancy. Apart from this abortive experiment with painting Stephen spent the time leading up to his move back to Cambridge resting, amusing himself at De Vere Gardens, and visiting his Cambridge friends.

Stephen had always liked clubs and debating and on 30 January 1891 the two came together when he founded the Walpole Debating Society. The inaugural meeting took place in his rooms, and amongst the founder members were Walter Headlam, Montague James, and Oscar Browning. A number of rules were agreed. The Society was for debating political, literary and social matters, there should be no membership fee (although this was altered to 6d (2p) to pay for print costs, at the second meeting), and there was a limit on how long each speaker could hold the floor. Also there was to be no restriction on drinking or smoking, that proper records of meetings be kept, and that membership should not exceed twenty five. W D Green was elected President and Oscar Browning was asked to present an address on Horace Walpole, after whom the club was named. Walpole's name was appropriate in view of his literary record and his connection with Eton and King's. However this modest request to Browning produced the club's first rift, and it had scarcely been in existence for an hour! For some reason Browning objected to speaking about Walpole and left the room. Perhaps he felt he should have been the President, but in any event, he did not return. The Society took a dim view of his behaviour, and as a punishment it was decided that he should oppose the Society's first debating motion a week later. Browning accepted this atonement and was faced with opposing a motion that had been one chosen by Stephen himself. It ran 'that the female sex stands in need of being repressed'. It was a proposal that did Stephen's reputation no good at all in subsequent discussions about his view of women. Predictably Browning lost the debate by ten votes to five, and was never seen in a Walpole Society meeting again.

Stephen's involvement in the Society was also short. He attended meetings regularly for four months during which time he debated such subjects as 'That it is the duty of every citizen to take an active interest in politics', which he opposed, and 'That Mr Booth's scheme of social salvation is likely to do more harm than good'. This time he voted in favour of the motion, which was won by six votes to two. William Booth's Salvation Army movement survived this result, and Stephen's own stricture, to become one of the most important social influences of the 20th century. Stephen's last appearance at the Society was on 15 May when he proposed 'That Darwin's theory as to the origin of species is not sufficiently well proved to justify its general acceptance'. The motion was carried by six votes to five. Both in respect of the Salvation Army and Charles Darwin's Origin of Species work, Stephen's views have subsequently been found wanting. Although Stephen's time with his brainchild was short, he had created a debating chamber that was long lived and properly run. It continued for twenty three years, and then on 20 February 1914 with the Great War looming, and after 352 meetings, the secretary brought it to a close with the words 'the Society then adjourned'. It had been a significant and well respected addition to university life.

However, back in the spring of 1891, all was not well in Stephen's mind. The previous year had been difficult for him, and Stephen was dissatisfied with himself. On 25 February, his birthday, he wrote to Oscar Browning telling him he was thirty-two that day and 'that nothing had been done for immortality'. He set about putting this right, but his days were numbered. His behaviour had been noticed by Arthur Clough, an old friend, fellow Apostle and member of the Duke of Clarence's inner circle. Clough wrote to Henry Smith, another colleague of Stephen on 19 March. Smith too was an Apostle and friend of the Duke:

> 'I saw Jim KS a good deal in Camb. He is far from sane, is about to publish his poetry, take a cottage in Madingley Road and stand for parliament. Poems of his (not very good ones) come out in the Pall Mall from time to time, and he is likely to publish a volume of all his works, except for the improper ones'.

The following month Stephen decided to visit Paris. This was at the same time that his father's retirement from the Bench was being finalised. For Sir James it was a difficult and emotional period. He might have hoped that the New Year would prove a calmer, happier time for the family, but this was certainly not to be the case. Sir James Stephen had been a friend of Robert Bulwer-Lytton better known as Lord Lytton, since the two had started corresponding over government policy in India. Lord Lytton had taken over as Viceroy in 1876, and Sir James had served as a legal member on the Viceregal Council from 1869 to 1872. Sir James was delighted at the attention Lord Lytton gave to his advice. He wrote:

> 'You have no conception of the pleasure which a man like me feels in meeting with one who really appreciates and is willing to make use of the knowledge which he had gained with great labour and much thought. You have managed to draw me out of my shell as no one ever else did'.

Later Sir James told Lord Lytton when the latter's Viceroyship was coming to an end:

> 'You are the only prominent public man who ever understood my way of looking at things. You have not only understood me, but in your warm hearted and affectionate way, exaggerated beyond measure the value of my sayings and doings'.

It has to be said that it was a carefully crafted piece of correspondence linking flattery with the self-congratulatory. Sir James realised that a close personal relationship with a senior peer whose career was bound to surpass his own, could be very useful. Sycophantic as it may have been, Sir James was to prove to have been remarkably canny when in 1887 Lord Lytton was appointed British Ambassador to France. Lord Lytton had always had his own artistic aspirations, and his poem Fables in Song had been generously reviewed by Robert Louis Stevenson. As Ambassador he often entertained Oscar Wilde in Paris.

The correspondence and friendship between Sir James and Lord Lytton had not wavered during the intervening years. It was then quite natural that when the procedure to force Sir James to leave the Bench was in its final stages, that Sir James's eldest son Herbert should write to Lord Lytton with details of his father's demeanour. Sir James was clearly upset that he had been required to resign and was looking for the best exit-strategy. Top of his list was a longing to be made a Privy Councillor, a honorary title given to the country's most distinguished civil servants on retirement, including by custom High Court judges. But there was a snag. Sir James had not served his full term as a judge, and therefore was not technically eligible for the award. Nevertheless he hoped for some flexibility in the application of the rules. The position carried with it great prestige and the entitlement to use the title Rt Hon. As Sir James had been a judge there was every chance that he would have been asked to serve on the Judicial Committee of the Privy Council.

On 6 April Herbert Stephen wrote to Lord Lytton. Extracts from his letter are as follows:

> 'My dear Lord Lytton,
>   You will see from tomorrow's papers that the judge's resignation is now practically accomplished. He goes down to the Lord's tomorrow to take leave of the Bar, and exchange complimentary speeches according to custom of retiring judges. It is very disagreeable and he dislikes it extremely, but I have no doubt whatever of its being the right thing to do. If he, the judge, is made a Privy Councillor as I expect he will be (though I myself don't think he expects so) it will go a long way towards making him quite happy'

The letter then went on to discuss the possibility of Sir James receiving the lesser title of baronetcy, but when he realised that there were about one thousand baronets already, his feeling was that it would 'turn the grape pretty sour if it proves to be'. That old ambition of the Stephen family would not be suppressed.

A week later Sir James's fears were confirmed and Herbert Stephen wrote again to Lord Lytton.

> 'My father, I think, has made up his mind – with disgust – that he will not be made a Privy Councillor after which very honorary distinction his soul yearned. I believe the particular compliment of having the other will satisfactorily prove to him his services have not been thought little of, and will please him as much again. As far as I am concerned I shall be satisfied

19. Talland House, the Stephens' holiday home in Cornwall (*Leslie Stephen*)

20. Virginia Woolf playing cricket with her brother Adrian in the garden of Talland House (© *Tate, London 2008*)

21. Walton Mill near Felixstowe, where Stephen was injured (*John Smith*)

22. Princes Edward and George on a visit to Australia in 1881. In the
centre, peering through, is a lookalike of Stephen (*John Murray*)

23. Stephen's rooms at Lincoln's Inn were at 3 Stone Buildings (*Andy and Sue Parlour*)

24. Eleanor Locker, one of Stephen's unsuccessful courtships. For a while she was married to one of Alfred Lord Tennyson's sons (*Tennyson Research Centre*)

25. Stella Duckworth, a cousin to Stephen and half sister to Virginia Woolf. Another of Stephen's unfulfilled hopes (*Charleston Trust*)

"The Reflector."

James Stephen.
Lonsdale Chambers.
27 Chancery Lane.
London. w.c. 22 Ap 1888

26. Stephen's letter to Oscar Browning confirming the demise of *The Reflector* after seventeen issues (*Gary A. Brown*)

27. Two watercolours completed by Stephen. Top: A self-portrait as a
visitor of the sick. Bottom: Oscar Browning in a similar role (© *2007 The*
Provost and Scholars of King's College, Cambridge)

28. Sir Leslie Stephen, uncle of
Stephen, and father of Virginia
Woolf (*The Savile Club*)

29. Lord Lytton, British
Ambassador to France at the time
of Stephen's brief imprisonment
in Paris (*The Savile Club*)

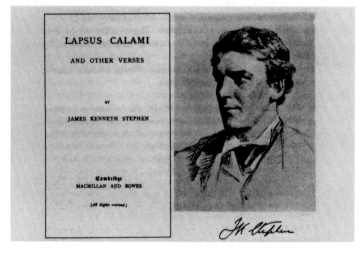

30. The frontispiece of Stephen's book of poems entitled *Lapsus Calami*
(*MacMillan and Bowes*)

31. The Blue Boar Inn, Cambridge. Stephen's base for tutoring undergraduates, and the scene of his arrest and committal to St. Andrew's Hospital (*Andy and Sue Parlour*)

32. St. Andrew's Hospital where Stephen died (*Andy and Sue Parlour*)

33. Stephen's gravestone in Kensal Green cemetery (*Andy and Sue Parlour*)

that his merits have been properly recognised. He was observing the other day that he had sat on five Royal Commissions, and considering how much of the work he did on all of them, there can be no doubt he deserves distinction'.

At the same time that Sir James was coping with the disappointment of compulsory retirement and the second prize of a baronetcy, something was going on that would have concerned him even more. During the first week in April, James Stephen, on holiday in Paris, was arrested and charged with 'escoperil'. This was a French term for fraud. It seems Stephen had been dashing about the city, spending wildly and refusing to pay the bills. He was locked up and spent twenty-four hours in prison. His first recourse was to his father's old friend Lord Lytton, who he knew was the British Ambassador and could therefore somehow secure his release. This Lord Lytton did but not before guaranteeing all the debts and claiming that Stephen was suffering a mental disorder as a result of an accident. Nevertheless it took considerable influence to win Stephen's freedom and to persuade the creditors to take no further action once there were assured of their money. By rescuing Stephen not only did Lord Lytton perform a great personal favour for Sir James, but he compounded it by omitting any reference to it in his weekly reports to the Foreign Office. These were quite detailed reports of what diplomatic events had occurred and the Stephen episode would normally have merited inclusion. Lord Lytton knew that this was a sensitive time for Sir James, and an uncomplimentary report about his son could have damaged any chance he had of appointment to the Privy Council. It was a generous omission. Stephen's father's long-term cultivation of Lord Lytton had borne a large fruit. No wonder when Lord

Lytton died in the following November, Sir James felt his death very deeply.

For someone as gregarious as Stephen, he had a strange streak of ungratefulness. On 14 April he wrote as follows to Lord Lytton from De Vere Gardens:

'Dear Lord Lytton,

My extreme anxiety to spare my Father any annoyance just now, leads me to appeal to you once more, and to implore you not to leave this letter unanswered and unacknowledged like its predecessor. What I ask of you is simply to say that upon the occasion to which I have referred you were mistaken and that you regret having stated, in good faith and with the best intentions, what ultimately turned out, in the official witness of three French doctors, to be untrue. If this letter is not answered, I must come to Paris and attempt in the first instance to obtain a personal interview with you, and with the Prefect of Police.

I am, Yours faithfully
J K Stephen'

As British Ambassador, Lord Lytton was under no obligation to reply to correspondence from people of Stephen's rank, especially if the letters were in any way threatening or uncivil. The fact that on 17 April he did so, was due entirely to his long term friendship with Stephen's father. Written from Cannes, the letter ran:

'Dear James Stephen,
In replying to your letter of the 14th inst it is true that on hearing of your arrest and imprisonment on a charge reported to me as one of escoperil, I informed the Prefect of Police at

Paris that I believed you to be suffering from the effects of an accident which at the time of the circumstances to which that charge related, had superinduced a condition of temporary cerebral excitement and disorder such as to render you for the time being unable to realise the character and consequences of your actions and for this reason I would be responsible for the repayment of the debts you had incurred in Paris, if the Prefect could induce your creditors, on that condition, to refrain from prosecuting the charge under which you were arrested. It is also true that the Prefect informed me after his receipt of that message, that the Director of the Prefecture had been unable to detect any trace of cerebral excitement and disorder in your reply to his questions.

I need hardly add that my statement to the Prefect was made by me in good faith, believing it to be true and with my best intentions on your behalf.

Yours faithfully
Lord Lytton

PS The above is all I can say and I must beg you to clearly understand that I cannot enter in a correspondence with you on this subject'.

The next day Sir James himself wrote to Lord Lytton. By this time he had come to terms with the award of a baronetcy, and, at least to Lord Lytton, had accepted it with a good grace. Also by now he had heard of his son's trouble in Paris. He did not attempt to understate the problem. Extracts from the letter read:

'32 De Vere Gardens
18 April 1891

My dear Lytton,
Just before I got your welcome letter, I received one from Salisbury announcing the baronetcy. It was very welcome. I

think it is an acknowledgement of work well done and deserving of a good mark as a badge on the coat of an old soldier. I am thoroughly pleased with the honour and glory as I shall be if I follow my father's example as to the PC (Privy Councillor) honour. I do not expect it as it is not the custom for it to be given to a judge who has not served his full time. Everybody has been kind about my retirement. I have been almost overwhelmed with kind and pleasant letters.

I shall not forget the kindness of your behaviour towards James, though I am afraid he still feels this mad resentment against you. He lives at Cambridge now as a general rule, though he continues to come up here to my regret and disgust. He has however now moved into a quiet condition and behaves like a rational person. It is one of the peculiar nuisances of his condition that he is quiet and rational enough between his different fits, but we can never tell when he will have another. He has now extravagantly wasted about £800-900 which I have paid – I do not know the exact amount, and which he had received in the most harsh and ungrateful way. In short I don't know whether the hypothosis of sanity or insanity is most dishonourable to him. I think each is equally bad for if he is insane it is for want of self-denial carried to an exaggerated pitch, and if he is not, his conduct is inexcusable. But this is enough upon the most odious and miserable of all subjects'

He signs off the letter:

'my dear fellow, Yours most affectionately and respectfully
J F Stephen'

On 21 April two more letters were making their way to the Ambassador's quarters. The first from Stephen to Lord Lytton in reply to the latter's letter dated 17 April. It was sent from King's College, Cambridge:

'Dear Lord Lytton,

    I gratefully acknowledge receipt of your letter which I am glad to have. I do not understand the reference to an 'accident' which is supposed to have befallen me. No such accident happened; nor did I ever suffer from 'cerebral excitement'. Your statement was I always knew made in good faith, though on ludicrously insufficient evidence; but it led to my incarceration for 24 hours in a small cell with a suicidal maniac, and has since done me great and irreparable harm.

I am, Yours faithfully
J K Stephen

PS Nothing is further from my wish than a correspondence with you. I asked for (and have obtained) a disavowal of an uninformed slander, otherwise likely to do me infinite damage. It was your fault I had to write four or five times'.

At the same time Herbert Stephen was writing to Lord Lytton from the Savile Club:

'My dear Lord Lytton,

It was a very generous act on your part to answer J's letter. I suppose by this time he has written again demanding to be informed who had made to you what statements upon which you based your absolutely erroneous assertions about him. I don't suppose you will answer such a demand, but if it would be in any way convenient to you to make use of anything I have said or wrote to you, by all means do. As to J coming to Paris, there is one (and only one) thing that I can and certainly shall do in the direction of preventing it, and that is to dissuade anybody I can from giving him for any purpose as much as £5 at once, without which he can't come, as railways, thank God, don't give credit terms to the younger sons of baronets'.

Herbert Stephen goes on to suggest that not to be made a Privy Councillor had been a blow to Sir James's self-esteem:

'I do think they might have stretched a point as to the PC. It is such a nuisance for him to dine with Jeunes (juniors) as he did last night and have to take down a gloomy stranger instead of Lady S. because there happens to be present a little chancery judge about 10 years his junior'.

As a postscript he added an intriguing question 'Do you know anything of the two alleged 'English Gentlemen' suggested to be MPs charged with unspeakable offences in Paris? Anything you can repeat I mean'.

Sir James had been in poor health for some years, and the events of April can only have hastened this decline. He had failed to be appointed a Privy Councillor, and he had had to admit that his son was probably mad. Thirdly he would have felt great embarrassment at the conduct of Stephen in Paris, especially because it involved Lord Lytton. His son's aggressive, surly letters and failure to acknowledge Lord Lytton's help in getting him released from prison would have been an anathema to him.

Chapter 15

An Indian Summer

From Stephen's point of view it was just another incident for which he blamed everyone except himself. He seemed oblivious to the embarrassment his predicament had caused his father. Nor had he any gratitude to his father for clearing his debts. Over a period these had amounted to, in today's values, over £40,000. Stephen's grip on reality was fading fast. It was at this point that it seems that the family became unnerved and tired of Stephen's behaviour. The three key people to take action would have been his father Sir James, his elder brother Herbert and his uncle Leslie. All realised the situation and other members of the family would have supported their views. Leslie Stephen's two daughters, Stella and Virginia would have been particularly keen that some restraint was put upon Stephen. What seems possible is that the three men told Stephen that the next time there was a serious incident, he could expect Dr Savage's recommendation to be enforced, and that he would have to go into secure accommodation. In 1891 this meant a hospital for the mentally ill – a lunatic asylum. Unfortunately Stephen's depression and mood swings were not something he could voluntarily control. To treat him as an errant schoolboy could never work in the long term. Nevertheless for whatever reasons, the next six months were the most productive and stable of Stephen's adult life.

Unperturbed by the trouble his antics in Paris had caused,

he set about organizing a dinner for the Old Eton Collegers in London. Stephen was the secretary of the Old Collegers, and the letter sent to Browning was dated 16 April. In it he asks prospective guests to attend a planning meeting 'at Mr F R Y Radcliffe's rooms 5 Hare Court, Temple at 4.30 pm next Thursday the 23rd inst.' It was an efficiently typed letter, personalised to 'O B'.

Stephen's next venture, still in April was to publish the first edition of Lapsus Calami, a slim volume of his verses. In May a second edition came out with some alterations, and in June a third. Stephen was surprised and delighted with the success of the book. In the preface to the June edition he wrote:

> 'It causes me real uneasiness to reflect that there are one thousand copies of Lapsus Calami loose about the land. The little volume contained much that was merely printed for the sake of having it in a permanent form, and much more that was only intended for the eyes of a select few. Had I anticipated so large a sale, and so general and friendly a notice from the newspaper press, I should have exercised a far more scrupulous discretion in selecting rhymes for publication. If everyone who bought an original Lapsus Calami buys a revised Lapsus Calami, and if everyone who did not buy the old one buys the new one, I shall be satisfied. J K S'

> Jemabad
> June 1891

The book starts with an address to C S Calverley, an earlier poet at Cambridge who Stephen admired, and tried to emulate. Much of Stephen's work and reputation stemmed from his love of parodying the great poets. Men such as Robert Browning, Lord Byron, Walter Scott, the American Walt Whitman, Robert Burns, Thomas Gray and even

Shakespeare were the respectful targets of his pen. When Browning died, Stephen issued a graceful apology in case his motives had been misunderstood. He called the verse 'A Parodist's Apology' It included the lines:

> 'If I've dared to laugh at you, Robert Browning,
> 'Tis with eyes that with you have often wept:
> You have oftener left me smiling or frowning,
> Than any beside, one bard except.
>
> But once you spoke to me, storm-tongued poet,
> A trivial word in an idle hour;
> But thrice I looked on your face and the glow it
> Bore from the flame of the inward power.'

Besides Calverley, Stephen dedicated poems to poets he esteemed such as Rudyard Kipling and to many of his friends including Walter Headlam, Arthur Benson, Arthur Clough, and Bernard Holland. In this way he personalised much of his work to people he liked either as poets or individuals.

Often his poetry was a spontaneous reaction to something he saw or felt, or to a social movement of the day. An example of this was a short poem called 'On the King's Parade'. Mashers and Swells were a fashion order that developed to replace the Regency dandies, although it was a less elevated social grouping. Sometimes it strayed into the middle classes. It was recognisable by smart, distinctive dress aimed to impress women. Its elegance was seen as pretentious in view of the group's social station, and it became the butt of music hall jokes. The Duke of Clarence was described as a 'Masher and Swell' on account of his characteristic high collars and wide cuffs, which earned him the nickname 'Collar and Cuffs'. He of course, did not fit the social stereotype, but it did suggest an element of fashion consciousness on his part to impress the ladies.

Stephen came across a 'Masher and Swell' at a railway station, and spent his journey penning the following:

> 'As I was waiting for a tardy train,
> I met what purported to be a man.
> What seemed to pass for its material frame,
> The semblance of a suit of clothes had on,
> Fit emblem of the grand sartorial art
> And worthy of a more sublime abode.
> Its coat and waistcoat were of weird design
> Adapted to the fashion's latest whim.
> I think it wore an Athenaeum tie.
> White flannels draped its too ethereal limbs
> And in its vacant eye there glared a glass'.

The June edition of Lapsus Calami included forty-eight poems and ninety-two pages. A fifth and last edition came out after his death in March 1892. The collection was revered amongst the boys at Eton who knew Stephen only by reputation. Once when the editor of the school magazine questioned the work, a furious member of the sixth form approached him and berated him with 'I suppose you will be criticising Tennyson next'. Another volume of verses, Quo Musa Tendis? , also came out in April 1891. This too was later republished.

Over the years Lapsus Calami has been recognised as a fine book of light verse. It is timeless and each successive generation has enjoyed and admired it. Different people over the years have had different favourite poems, but the general level is recognised as being high. Today the book is still popular and a copy can easily be obtained. It has stood the test of time. The Oxford Dictionary of Quotations carries four of Stephen's verses, including one from Lapsus Calami, a tribute to Wordsworth:

> 'Two voices are there: one is of the deep;
> It learns the storm-cloud's thunderous melody,
> Now roars, now murmurs with the changing sea,
> Now bird-like pipes, now closes soft in sleep:
> And one is of an old half-witted sheep
> Which bleats articulate monotony,
> And indicates that two and one are three,
> That grass is green, lakes are damp and mountains steep
> And, Wordsworth, both are thine'.

Lapsus Calami was Stephen's one real lasting legacy. Even in the preface Stephen could not resist a joke. He signs off from 'Jemabad' – a place whose whereabouts have defeated the India Office Library, the National Geographical Society and several gazetteers. It can only be a place invented by Stephen to incorporate his nickname. Unfortunately Stephen was not always to have the last laugh.

Stephen had moved back to Cambridge in the spring and he may have realised that this was his last chance to live a structured normal life. He took some rooms at the Blue Boar Inn in Trinity Street with the intention of earning an income by taking students for private tuition. To do this he placed an advertisement in the Cambridge Review on 14 May which read:

> 'Mr J K Stephen M A, late Fellow of King's College coaches gentlemen for all Law and History examinations and prepares candidates for the Whewell Scholarships. Several vacancies for this Term and the Long Vacation – apply to 18 Trinity Street'.

A similar advertisement appeared the following October.

It was at this time that Stephen coined the phrase 'the intellectual aristocracy'. It was born out of Stephen's belief that 'intellectual' was a measure of mental and moral attributes, not dependent on money or birth. The 'aristocracy' part came from a rather smug certainty that because of their intellects, the members were safe in their social superiority. They considered themselves a race apart from the real aristocracy, and did not want to be confused with the nobility or ruling classes. What Stephen had devised was not far from the Bloomsbury philosophy a decade later.

The summer months passed well for Stephen. He was at home in a university environment, amongst friends old and new. His debating skills at the Union and intellectual talents were admired, and even his health seemed to improve. Lincoln's Inn records show that he took up new rooms at 27 Chancery Lane, so he may even have thought of trying to revive the dying embers of a legal career. In any event in July he wrote to Browning asking if he would 'conscientiously testamonalize me for a readership in Roman Law jurisprudence and International Law'. There is no sign that this ambition came to anything. On 24 September Stephen again wrote to Browning 'Blessed is the man who writes a letter unprovoked and therefore blessed are you and moreover blessed am I. I've enjoyed my holidays very much and look forward keenly to next term'. Browning was impressed with Stephen's renaissance. He commented 'In the summer he became quite well, and in October I found him looking healthier than I had ever seen him. He is full of energy and hope'. Such assessments gave promise that Stephen was at last achieving some degree of stability that satisfied him, but two poems in the Spectator suggested that doubts remained. It was the proposal that a tennis court be built in the College garden that triggered

Stephen's anger, which he expressed in his poem 'The Fellows' Garden'. This was published in the Spectator, as was the reply on 22 August from an unidentified EDS. It was a lengthy work and its gist was to sympathise with Stephen's frustrations, whilst advising calmness, and reflection. Its mood was summed up in these lines:

'Thy wrath is just, but is it wise
To fume and fret, to stamp and splutter,
When prudence bids thee temporise
And smoothly spread the melting butter?
Just humour him with kindly greeting,
When next the College holds a meeting'

The old demons had not gone away completely. It was during this period of apparent rejuvenation that Stephen decided to form what he called 'the Coffee Club'. He liked a cup of coffee after lunch, and the format was that there were six members who took it in turns to provide coffee in their rooms, usually on a Sunday. The six original members were Oscar Browning, Walter Headlam, Nathaniel Wedd, Marcus Dimsdale, Montague James and Stephen. One of Stephen's favourite amusements at these get-togethers was recorded years later in the issue of The Academy dated 19 August 1905. 'He used to divert the company by asking them for authors of quotations; he would quote rapidly and without effort and they would guess. Often after a unanimous cry of 'Wordsworth' or 'Browning', he would say quickly 'No J K S' When Stephen died the club lived on in his memory. Once when the coffee was brought in, the remark was made 'Poor Mr Stephen! It always reminds me of the Sacrament'.

It was in October that Stephen achieved another personal success. A controversy had arisen within Cambridge on whether some knowledge of Greek should continue to be a necessary qualification for a degree. Stephen opposed the change and published a fifty page pamphlet called The Living Language. It was a most accomplished paper, setting out lucid and persuasive arguments for the retention of Greek. This was not just an internal argument amongst the academics of the university, anxious to pontificate their own views, it took on something of a national debate. The Times devoted a hundred column inches to the discussion in their letters page over two days. Stephen's views contained in The Living Language were backed up in his own letter to the paper on 28 October:

'To the Editor of the Times

Sir, As you have devoted some attention to the question which is to form the subject of a vote of the Senate next Thursday at Cambridge you will perhaps allow me to say for the benefit of those of your readers who are non-resident graduates of this question which is being brought forward by the opponents of Greek at the last moment almost to the exclusion of all other considerations.

We are told that the resistance to the grace to be proposed on Thursday is resistance to inquiry and can only be based on a narrow dogmatism, which refuses to look facts in the face, for fear they should prove fatal to it. The answer is simple. The facts have been looked in the face. Such evidence as that of which we are asked for facilitate the collection has been collected. It has been printed, circulated, rendered accessible to every one, and carefully considered. The University has twice decided in the light of all procurable information, to retain Greek as a compulsory subject in the Little-go; and if it is urged that some years have elapsed since the last decision it can be answered that it is only two years since every question relevant to the present issue was discussed in connexion with the retention of Greek in the Poll degree.

The aggressive and irrepressible spirit of opposition to classical studies which has led to the present attempt to re-open a closed question would alone justify the supporters of Greek in the attitude they have taken up. Moreover the composition of the Syndicate is such as to render the proposal in the eyes of many residents, a distinct challenge to the advocates of Greek to regard the present grace as a test question on which pitched battle ought to be fought. The advocates of 'fair play' and 'freedom of inquiry' are aware of these facts and are aware that they are known to all residents. They would be the first, if the grace were passed, to point to the vote as practically conclusive to the main question at issue. It is, therefore, only fair that the facts which I have mentioned should be present to the minds of non-resident voters.

I am, Sir, your obedient servant.

J K Stephen
18, Trinity Street
Oct 25'

Stephen's letter may seem long-winded, but by the standards of the day it was concise.

It took a Walter Wren some two thousand words to express his support for Stephen's argument that Greek should be retained as an obligatory subject. Wren's letter must be a contender for the longest letter ever published by The Times. On the same day Henry Sidgwick, an old friend of Oscar Browning and a pillar of Cambridge life sent to The Times a letter signed by fifteen of the University's professors and three heads of Colleges also opposing the change. As might be expected Herbert Stephen weighed in with support for his brother. Part of his letter read:

'This new meaning of the word 'education' has been lately set out at length by, amongst others, Mr J K Stephen in a pamphlet entitled The Living Language (Macmillan and Bowes) and I most heartily agree with what is there said on the subject'.

Two other friends of Oscar Browning, who had accompanied him on various outings to Europe over the years, added their objections to the change. They were Richard Jebb and James Welldon. Jebb went abroad with Browning three times between 1873 and 1877. Once to the Alps, and twice to Italy. Browning recalled that Jebb's letters to him were always signed 'Yours affectionately' or with 'some stronger expression of feeling'. Browning had met up again with Jebb at Cambridge through Stephen. Stephen had been entertaining Jebb to tea in his rooms when in came Browning. He observed 'a small elegant person with side whiskers, smoking a cigar', but Browning enjoyed his conversation, and the friendship was resumed. Jebb was a distinguished Greek scholar, so his opposition to the proposal was to be expected. He even quoted support from Sir William Thomson, President of the Royal Society. 'He is amongst those who hold that Greek ought to remain a necessary subject for the Cambridge degree in arts. He agrees very heartily with the reasons against such as Syndicate'. In characteristic Cambridge style there was even a committee formed to oppose the motion. It was called the 'Executive Committee for Opposing the Grace'. Jebb and Welldon were both members. Browning had known Welldon since he 'recruited' him from the brother's school at Thorpe Mandeville. He too was fluent in Greek, and the two would read passages of Plato together during their tours.

The Times printed one or two letters in favour of the change, but these were swamped by the level of opposition.

On Thursday 29 October the vote duly took place, and the result was a resounding victory for the retention of Greek. For Stephen and for most of the senior staff at Cambridge it was a triumph. Stephen had gone to the trouble to publish a most convincing and readable pamphlet. It would certainly have influenced the Senate. Stephen's contribution was fully recognised. He was viewed as the leader of the campaign and received most of the plaudits. His stock at Cambridge had never been higher.

One man who wrote a very favourable review of the pamphlet was Evelyn Shuckburgh. His aunt had been a granddaughter of Charles Dickens, and he was a master at Eton during Stephen's time there. His classical credentials were first class. He had won the First Classical Tripos at Emmanuel College, Cambridge and become the examiner in Latin and Greek at Edinburgh University. From someone of this background, fifteen years older than Stephen, his approval was highly valued. Stephen felt he had to acknowledge Shuckburgh's review:

'Oct 22 1891

Dear Shuckburgh

I don't like appearing in the capacity of a writer thanking a reviewer when I can help it, because such thanks might be taken to imply that the review was partly due to personal considerations. I hope you won't draw any such inference if I don't deny myself – for I can't – the satisfaction of saying how much pleasure your notice of my Greek pamphlet has given me. I have the misfortune of not being always taken seriously, the unhappy peculiarity of occasionally making a joke when a joke is not expected. I was honestly apprehensive of what my critics would say. Quite apart from its specially kindly and appreciative tone, your treatment of the pamphlet as a solid and serious contribution to the controversy has been a distinct relief and a real delight to me.

Yours sincerely
J K Stephen'

The letter reveals a side of Stephen's character not seen before. It was far from the arrogance of the 'intellectual aristocracy', indeed he seemed genuinely nervous at the reception his pamphlet would have, and was delighted when it was favourable. An element of self-doubt amongst the usual intellectual certainty of university scholars, was refreshing. He was also perceptive enough to be aware that perhaps he should not be thanking Evelyn Shuckburgh at all. It was the letter of a modest man, thrilled by the approval.

Chapter 16

Decline and Fall

Despite his Senate success, there were signs that depression was beginning to set in during early November. There was a pattern in his behaviour, which suggested that times of success or enjoyment did not necessarily increase his stability. Several years earlier at the Duke of Clarence's twenty-first birthday party at Sandringham, Harry Wilson had noted in his diary that Stephen was 'strangely quiet'. In the circumstances he should have been at the top of his form. Periods of great energy and enthusiasm were sometimes followed by inertia causing him to lose interest in work, and in more mundane matters such as finding his own home in Cambridge. Browning noticed this marked change.

'His face assumed a look of depression, while all around him were talking, generally he was the most animated of the group. He became still more dull. At last he confined himself to his rooms in Trinity Street where he sat day after day, scarcely speaking, reading or indeed eating'. The terrible spectre of depression had returned, and it was not to go away.

Meanwhile life for the new Duke of Clarence was becoming enjoyable. He was combining an army career, which took him out of London for much of the time, and a round of royal duties. Some gave him pleasure, some he found rather dull, but he was coping well with his demotion. Then in October to his parents' great relief a suitable person was found for him to marry. Princess May the daughter of the Duke and Duchess of Teck was called to Balmoral. Although the Tecks were on the fringes of the royal family, they were not well off, indeed the Duchess was popularly known as the Duchess of Tick, so the chance to marry into the heart of the family was never going to be rejected. At Balmoral Queen Victoria approved of May and declared her to be 'a solid girl, which we want. She has no frivolous tastes and has been very carefully brought up'. Princess May and the Duke had less chance to pass judgment on each other. It was implied by their families that this was their duty in the interests of the monarchy, so the formal courtship was under way. To mark the match the Duke was promoted to lieutenant colonel.

In the middle of November before the engagement had been formally announced he wrote to Stephen in Cambridge telling him of the impending good news. Stephen had been unaware of these developments and the letter must have come as a shock. He was already in a state of depression, and the Duke's letter was the final straw. Something in his brain was triggered by the realisation that finally the Duke was lost to him. Perhaps memories of their relationship at Cambridge eight years earlier resurrected a latent jealously. Although he had seen little of the Duke in recent years, his mind still harked back to the time when the Duke was almost his property. As Theo Aronson put it in his book, Prince Eddy and the Homosexual Underworld, Stephen 'began to look back on their time together as a sort of idyll'. Six months of success and stability were finally blown away by the news. Barely three weeks after his triumph in the Senate, Stephen had suddenly slipped beyond repair. The Duke had written to Stephen at 18 Trinity Street; Stephen's reply came from the violent ward of St Andrew's Hospital, Northampton.

On 21 November, exactly a year after Dr Savage had written his recommendation that Stephen should be confined, and a day or two after receiving the Duke's engagement letter, the denouement came. Perhaps maddened by his depression and by jealousy for his lost Duke, he threw a violent and sustained fit in his room. He was found by his landlady and his Cambridge doctor Lawrence Humphrey, was called.

Dr Humphrey's report tells of the chaos he found.

'Extreme depression – often declining to speak or answer questions. This morning I found him standing naked in his bedroom, smiling. All the furniture and clothes in disorder and in the street were the fragments of looking glass, which he had thrown out of the window. He has had attacks of depression lasting for some months, followed by periods of unusual excitability: communicated by Harry Lushington Stephen, 32 De Vere Gardens, London, Barrister at Law. This morning in an attack of violence he threw his looking glass out of the window into the street and stood naked in his room declining to move. Was under a delusion that there was a warrant out for his detention'.

Lawrence Humphrey M D

It was the moment his family had dreaded. Herbert Stephen was called and convinced Stephen that they were going for a pleasant outing in the country. The 'outing' ended up at St Andrew's Hospital. James Stephen was in a lunatic asylum, detained under an emergency order.

On admittance Stephen was assessed. He was not thought to be suicidal or dangerous, and there was no record of family insanity. It was also believed that this was his first serious attack, and that he had never received treatment. Some of this information, probably supplied by Herbert Stephen, was questionable. His own father had recently been stood down from the Bench with a brain disorder, and there had been several instances of Stephen's uncontrolled behaviour. Stephen's general medical condition was quite good. He was described as well built and muscular with no signs of recent injury or disease, and his heart and lungs were sound. Only his teeth needed attention. It was his behaviour that was disturbing. He was reluctant to bath in front of the doctors, and claimed there was nothing wrong with him except constipation. For this he was given opium. Otherwise he was very quiet and went to bed on his first night without further trouble.

The following day his brother Henry came to see him in the morning and the two had breakfast together. Stephen hardly spoke and gave only monosyllabic answers to questions. He took walks in the hospital garden or prowled about his room, and only showed aggression when an attendant tried to undress him for bed in the evening. On 23 November two more doctors came to assess him. The first G. H. Percival described him as 'very depressed, wanders disorderly about and will not amuse or interest himself in anything. Obstinately refuses to answer any question or to enter into conversation. He has delusions that there is a plot against him to deprive him of his liberty'. The second doctor, Arthur Milligan, said much the same but added that Henry Stephen had told him that his brother 'has for three years been subject to attacks and loss of self control, followed by fits of depression and inaction'.

For the next three weeks there was little change in Stephen. He continued to be very taciturn, sometimes ignoring questions completely, but the violence had subsided. This passive behaviour may, of course, have been induced by drugs to render him quiet and harmless and to help him come to terms with his new environment. He was eating better, and only the constipation continued to bother him. Although still very unsociable he would go for walks with his attendant, spend time reading, and write regularly to the Duke. It may have been due to drugs, but Stephen did show signs of settling down to a very controlled existence. This 'progress' continued through the first week in January. The hospital reported an improvement in his condition, he had taken to playing billiards and was exercising more. Then on 9 January he was visited by his mother, Lady Stephen, after which his mood changed. It is not clear why this was, but it is possible she told him that the Duke of Clarence was extremely ill with pneumonia and not expected to live. It would have been a natural subject for conversation, and could explain why Stephen immediately became quite different. He became irritable, he abandoned his walks and his reading and he hardly ate anything. He would pace up and down his room all day, not speaking, and once he threw his constipation pills into the fire. When the Duke's death was announced on 14 January, it was the final blow. Stephen from then on refused all food, which meant a feeding tube had to be used. To counter this he would not open his mouth and struggled so aggressively that he had to be fed through his nose. Laxatives were not working for his constipation, so he was given an enema. It was the middle of winter yet he would not allow his fire to be lit, and he had started to attack the attendants. He was in a terrible downward spiral, perhaps brought on by news of the Duke.

If Stephen was now out of sight to his friends, he was not out of their minds. On 20 January the Duke's funeral took place at Windsor. It had all the trappings of a State occasion with gun carriages, military uniforms for the men, and pall bearers from the 10th Hussars regiment. The weather prevented the Queen from attending. She sent a floral tribute and the message 'a mark of tenderest affection and love from his most devoted, loving and sorrowing grandmother, Victoria R I'. Tennyson wrote the anthem for the funeral:

> 'Life's dream is past,
> All its sin, its sadness.
> Brightly at last,
> Dawns a day of gladness'.

Amongst all the dignatories a small group of the Duke's Cambridge colleagues had been invited to the inner sanctum of the choir area of St George's Chapel, a place reserved only for the closest or most distinguished of the Duke's friends. The group consisted of Harry Wilson, Henry Goodhart, and Harry Cust. Wilson recorded the occasion 'we were not without a thought for poor Jim Stephen who would certainly have been with us if fate had not stricken him too, though in a different way. I need not say we were proud of the honour done us'.

By now Stephen was having to be fed three times a day by nasal tube, only enemas had any effect on his constipation, possibly caused by drug treatment, and he had become incontinent. His mother had sent him three letters, but he opened none of them. Something had happened during her visit ten days earlier that made him reject her completely. On 30 January it was reported that he was refusing food, and still had to be fed through his nose, yet he was just about surviving. Two days later he collapsed. The hospital fed him a little brandy, some eggs, tea and beef extracts, but he was hardly alive. The end came on 3 February. He had continued to receive the same diet as the day before. He was so weak he did not resist being fed by mouth, and the staff knew he was slipping away. His two brothers, Herbert and Henry, and his mother were summoned, and at 2.00 am they arrived. They talked for a while, then twelve hours later Stephen lost consciousness and died shortly after 4.00 pm. His mother, the two brothers and two attendants were present. The hospital records show that 'James Kenneth Stephen died at 4.22 pm in the presence of Edwin Cave, Chief Attendant. The cause of death being: Mania, Refusal of food, Exhaustion'.

Stephen was buried in Kensal Green cemetery on 6 February, alongside his grandparents and other family members. His father was to join him two years later. The funeral was kept discreet and private. Only family and a few friends from Cambridge attended, and no reports of it appeared in the national or local press. Stephen's gravestone can still be seen today. He shares a grave with one of his sisters, Margaret, who died in infancy, a brother Leslie who also died similarly young, and Frances whose funeral Stephen had attended twelve years earlier. There are three other Stephen family graves nearby.

For a man who was so careless of money, it was a small success that he managed to die solvent. If there had been any debts his father would quietly have cleared them, so the records show that Stephen died with a credit balance of £87. Tributes came in from national and local newspapers and from magazines with which Stephen had been associated. The Times spoke of his 'wit and wisdom', and described him as 'an eternal undergraduate'. The St James's Gazette said that 'literature has sustained a loss of performance and promise'. It also published a poem in Stephen's memory by Bernard Holland, which included the lines:

'Sweet vanished hours! Undying yet
In memory's inmost cell,
When we forget them we'll forget
Thee, dearest Jem, as well'.

The Speaker said of him 'a most striking personality, a genial companion and a witty conversationalist. The sense of mastery with which Calverley impresses us is one of his chief charms'. Stephen's local paper, the West London Reporter, carried a notice referring to his 'exceptionally brilliant talents' and the promise of a 'dazzling future'. Lastly, and perhaps appropriately, it was left to Oscar Browning in a long article in the Bookman in March 1892 to describe him as 'one of the best and most gifted spirits'. A selection of the tributes, or extracts from them, are included in the Appendices to this book under 'In Memoriam'.

His college friends put up a brass in his memory in the King's College chapel, and there is one in the chapel at Eton. The inscription on it reads:

'Quali per novissimos annos abundans
amore neminem sibi non devinxerit'

Loosely translated this means:

'His happy childhood made him always believe the best in everyone'

It may have been this philosophy, based partly on naivety and an over-indulged youth that later led through to disillusionment and depression. The author of this tribute was Hugh Macnaghten who was connected with Eton for fifty years, as pupil, master and administrator. By a curious co-incidence he was the nephew of Sir Melville Macnaghten, the Chief Constable of the Metropolitan Police, and it was he who put together some notes in 1894 accusing Stephen's old friend, Montague Druitt of the Ripper murders. A brass for another of his friends, Henry Goodhart also rests in the chapel at Eton. When Goodhart was elected a Fellow of his Cambridge College, Trinity, he told Stephen 'They have made me a Fellow, amongst other things'. Stephen who shared Goodhart's delight, suppressed his excitement with the reply 'what other things?'

At their country home in Ireland at Anaverna, the family put up a fountain in Stephen's memory. His father added a drinking cup as his own special tribute, and on 25 October 1892 was the first to drink from it. He never visited Anaverna again. For the Stephen family to lose a son in these circumstances would have been horrifying enough, but with their social ambitions, the stigma of madness was intolerable. It was made worse by Stephen's brilliant potential, and his almost universal popularity. For Sir James and Lady Stephen this was the fourth of their children that they had had to bury. In his book Leslie Stephen wrote:

> 'My nephew, Jim, a wonderfully promising lad, of whom I was very fond, died this spring under most melancholy circumstances. His father Fitzjames lives, but he is a changed man'.

It was salt into Sir James's wounds that his son had died on the fourth anniversary of the death of his closest friend Henry Maine.

From hospital notes, it is evident that only Stephen's mother visited him. His brothers brought him to St Andrew's, and sat by his deathbed. There was no mention of his father. The notes are detailed and a visit would have been a 'highlight' to be recorded. Perhaps the idea of seeing what they had condemned Stephen to, was too much for the three senior family members.

Stephen was remembered for a long time by that generation of royalty. In May 1900, the Prince of Wales, soon to be King Edward VII attended a dinner in London to mark the publication of the Directory of National Biography, a huge work, which Leslie Stephen had co-edited with Sidney Lee. Stephen was presented to the Prince who recalled that 'dear Jim had coached my son one long vacation'. The Prince was impressed with the Biography and on becoming monarch the following year the King offered Leslie Stephen a knighthood. At first, he claimed, he felt he should decline the honour as he considered himself as a 'literary gent', unworthy. However in the best Stephen family tradition, he soon overcame this modesty, and on the basis that it would be churlish to refuse, he duly accepted. The contrast in outcomes of the lives of uncle and nephew could scarcely be greater.

Chapter 17

'One Crowded Hour of Glorious Life is worth an Age without a Name'

Thomas Osbert Maudaunt 1730–1809

There can be no doubt that Stephen had a disorder of some sort, but it may not necessarily have been a brain defect. Over the years seven doctors had passed him fit. In 1887 Dr Gull is alleged to have said that he was 'completely cured' after the Felixstowe accident. Then in 1890 three doctors appointed by Dr Savage reported no malfunction of the brain, and finally in April 1891, three French doctors said the same. All these men were well qualified to detect any abnormality. Even Dr Humphrey in his report for Stephen's admission to St Andrew's Hospital talked of 'extreme depression', and not a brain illness. No qualified doctor who actually examined Stephen claimed that his brain was damaged. Today it would seem that Stephen was suffering from cyclothymia, a personality disorder, which causes severe mood swings between great excitement and great depression, between action and inertia. This could now be treated by psychotherapy, but in the late 1800s this was in its infancy. More serious was the threat of manic-depressive psychosis and Stephen could have been moving towards this. The family knew that something was seriously wrong with Stephen, but it seems medical science could not distinguish between personality and brain disorders. Cyclothymia can sometimes be traced back to genetic faults, particularly in bright, talented families. There were plenty of examples of this amongst Stephen's relations, before and after his death. It was

Stephen's misfortune that he inherited a condition which could not be properly diagnosed or treated.

In his prime Stephen had the potential as a parodist, wit and speaker to bear comparison with his contemporary Oscar Wilde. Nothing is known of any personal relationship, but Stephen did put Wilde up for membership of the Savile Club. Desmond MacCarthy compared the two in his book 'Portraits'. He wrote, 'both men loved to tumble about the convictions of others, while remaining very sentimental about anything they took seriously themselves, yet no two wits could have been more different. JKS was Philistine to the backbone; in laughter, strength, impulse, he was violently masculine, a lover of law and abstract arguments. Yet how well it suited both men to be giants with a surplus of raw vitality'. It was a mighty, but deserved, compliment to bracket Stephen in any literary respect with Wilde.

His old friend and admirer Arthur Benson put forward an original opinion on how Stephen might have overcome his state of mind. 'I think' wrote Benson, 'that the love of some wise and devoted woman would have given him much of what he stood most in need'. Such a woman never featured in his life, and when he imagined he had found such love, maybe twice, he was summarily rejected. By then it was probably too late anyway to make any difference. As it was he died frustrated and unfulfilled, a ruthless victim of a genealogical problem, which became known as 'the curse of the Stephens'.

A selection of the letters that Stephen wrote, from his days at Eton until a few weeks before he was sent to St Andrew's Hospital, were shown to one of the country's leading graphologists Elaine Quigley, who is also a psychologist. She had no previous knowledge of Stephen's personality. Mrs Quigley was able to conclude personality characteristics from the handwriting, rather than from a study of the words themselves.

The earliest letter that Mrs Quigley looked at was written by Stephen from Eton to Oscar Browning in October 1876. She saw evidence of a nervous, energetic character with fluctuating confidence who was not quite as extrovert as he would like to be believed. Although pleasant on the surface, there were indications of bad temper. To a great extent this view fits in with contemporary reports about Stephen's behaviour, and suggests that even at the age of seventeen, the essence of his personality was set. The next of Stephen's writings concerned his long report written in August 1883 about the progress of the Prince under his tutelage at Sandringham. Here signs of depression and inner anger showed through. Whilst he was a good talker and wanted to achieve results, he could be impatient and cynical. The mixture of anger and sensitivity may have been due to unsettling events when he was young which marred his emotional development. This probably related back to his relationship with his parents.

The third letter written to his sister Rosamund in January 1885, recalled the day of the Prince's 21st birthday. Here Mrs Quigley again found an explosive anger and resentment within him, and a personality far from being brash and confident was really quite brittle. He needed emotional support (and again this may go back to his mother), and had a poor understanding of women. He preferred to live hand to mouth with little regard for the future. Like Oscar Wilde, he would pick up new ideas, follow them enthusiastically, and then suddenly lose interest, although Stephen may have had a greater sense of responsibility than Wilde. It was as if he had forces within him, and every so often they became out of control.

The next letter was written in May 1887 when Stephen was

the secretary of the Social and Political Education League, and the tidy almost copperplate writing suggested that he was performing as requested within defined boundaries. Someone, probably Judge Lock, had applied a discipline to him, to which he could respond, although he did not like it. He seemed to doubt that anyone would listen to him, so he believed he lacked power to influence – another frustration that might go back to childhood. The letter was a performance for a purpose, and he disliked this constraint. Although the subject matter in these letters differs, a definable personality is showing through with some consistency.

The letter to Oscar Browning about the demise of The Reflector in April 1888 suggested he was now tired of the magazine, and just wanted to be rid of it. A huge ambition a few weeks earlier had now become a millstone and Stephen's inability to operate commercially was mostly to blame. He could not balance between what he wanted to do and what he ought to do. This made him resentful, and stubborn, although there was no denying his underlying intelligence. He was becoming a weird and fatal mixture.

The three letters Stephen wrote to Stella Duckworth towards the end of 1890 were meant to be love letters of a kind, but the writing itself showed no passion and they suggest he was going through some obligatory ritual, in which he did not really believe. Most of the characteristics shown in previous letters were repeated here. The scrawled envelope containing his outraged letter to the Savile Club simply showed that by this time he was falling apart. The last letter to Evelyn Shuckburgh perhaps indicated how other people could bring out the best in him. The writing was lively and interested, but there were signs that he was too weak mentally to pursue causes once they had started to go wrong.

Mrs Quigley's overall conclusion from examining the ten letters was that on the positive side was a sense of integrity, justice and urgency, and that he could be pleasant and articulate. On the other hand he felt perceived unfairness very deeply and he would cut off his nose to spite his face. Hence the great internal anger and frustration. He needed the freedom to control projects and then he could rise to the occasion and handle people well. He had little regard for material things such as clothes, money or accommodation. Today he might be ferreting around car boot sales for the essentials of life. Perhaps he needed someone to rely on, so Arthur Benson's suggestion that he needed 'the love of some wise and devoted woman' may not have been so outlandish after all.

There is much in Mrs Quigley's opinions that fits uncannily with the views of writers who had first hand knowledge of Stephen such as his temper, short-lived enthusiasms and disinterest in material and monetary needs. The influence, or lack of it, of his mother during childhood may have been a key formative factor. His great popularity with his contemporaries arose from his enthusiasm, his persuasiveness, and what they saw as leadership qualities. He was fun to be with and perhaps they neither realised nor cared if this façade masked a flawed and somewhat superficial character. Whatever his faults, the fact that he received so many glowing tributes after his death, including one fifty years later, underlines that his was a valued and significant life.

James Stephen should be remembered today as a fine poet, whose work compared with the best. He had the foresight to publish Lapsus Calami and Quo Musa Tendis?, so that, in his own words, they would be 'in a permanent form'. Nor are his efforts lost on today's generation. The current New Oxford Book of Victorian Verse includes seven of his poems. Two relate to 'England and America', three are soliloquies which make up 'After the Golden Wedding', and then there is the misogynistic 'In the Backs'. The last is 'A Remonstrance', written in 1891, and may have been written out of frustration at his rejection by Stella Duckworth. The first and last verses run:

> 'Love is what lacks then: but what does it mean to you?
> Where did you hear of it, feel it or see?
> What has the truth or the good of it been to you?
> How love some other, yet nohow love me?
>
> You dream a priceless love: I feel a penny one
> My reason plods, while your fancy can range:-
> Therefore, I ask, since you'll never love any one,
> Why should you not marry me for a change?'

Kingsley Amis, who chose the works included in the New Oxford Book of Light Verse, selected six of Stephen's poems. These were 'On a Parisian Boulevard', 'On a Rhine Steamer', 'Drinking Song', 'Sincere Flattery', 'A Sonnet' and 'To RK' (Rudyard Kipling). In the last of these he concluded with the lines:

> 'When Rudyards cease from kipling
> And the Haggards Ride no more'

It is to Stephen's credit that he has such a substantial input into modern and distinguished anthologies of poetry. The librarian at Stephen's old club, the Savile, can quote without effort from this poetry and his little books are still available at the press of an internet button. Of all the extended Stephen family, he arguably left a more memorable legacy than any of them, save for Virginia Woolf. His father was a moderately successful judge, both his brothers made good careers at law. One of them, Henry, followed in his father's footsteps to India and became a High Court judge from 1901 to 1914. He married a niece of Florence Nightingale and produced a son he named James. James too was afflicted by 'the curse' and spent several years in an asylum. Stephen's sister Katherine became the Principal of Newnham College at Cambridge. His uncle Leslie made a lasting mark with his prodigious Dictionary of National Biography, a worthy work of great usefulness. But the flair, the fun, the eccentricity and ultimately the tragedy belonged to Stephen. He did, as he wished, achieve a degree of immortality in different spheres. At Eton a toast to his name is still drunk after the annual Wall Game by the Collegers, and there is a brass plaque in the chapel. At Cambridge Walter Headlam, Oscar Browning and Henry James raised money for a plaque in King's Chapel. It was designed by Charles Ashbee, a noted architect and graduate of King's. He was the son of Henry Ashbee, who built an enormous collection of erotic books in the 1870s. It is also suspected that he was the subject of a semi-pornographic autobiography written by an anonymous 'Walter', called 'My Secret Life'.

Oscar Wilde knew of Ashbee's work and commented 'a dirty mind is a perpetual feast'. The literature is still the subject of interest today. Also at Cambridge Charles Furse's oil painting has a place of honour in the Combination Room, but it was as a poet of light verse that he is truly remembered. Not even bizarre suggestions that he was Jack the Ripper, can detract from his real status.

Fifty years after the day of his death, The Times issued a major commemorative tribute. It chose one of Stephen's own poems called 'Battle' to remember him by:

'But if I could have what some prayed for,
One more life to live how and when I chose,
I would ask to belong to one age when wrong
Is punished by honest unflinching blows,
When to hate's to fight in the open light,
And a dire offence is as direly paid for'

William Shakespeare, who Stephen had the nerve and the skill to parody, might have chosen these lines from his 'Midsummer Night's Dream' to summarise Stephen's life:

'Swift as a shadow, short as any dream
Brief as lightening in the collied night.'

Stephen would have been pleased and proud that appropriate words had been found from England's greatest dramatist and poet to celebrate his life.

Appendices

i. IN MEMORIAM

This is a collection of the obituaries and tributes made to James Stephen after his death.

The Times – 5th February 1892

'We regret to announce the death in his 33rd year of Mr James Kenneth Stephen MA, the younger son of Sir James Fitzjames Stephen. Mr Stephen was educated at Eton and at King's College, Cambridge, where he obtained the Members' Prize in 1880 and the Whewell Scholarship in 1881, and, after taking his degree with a first class in the Historical Tripos and a second in the Law Tripos, he was elected a Fellow of his college. For a short time he was tutor to his Royal Highness the late Prince Albert Victor during his residence at Cambridge. Few men have left behind them, at school or college, a greater reputation for brilliant ability than Mr Stephen, whose sayings and writings used to be quoted at Cambridge and at Eton with keen appreciation. After coming to London he started the Reflector, a weekly newspaper, and during its brief existence he himself wrote most of its articles – clever, original, and wayward compositions, which unluckily failed to command a sufficient audience. More recently he published two little volumes of poems, chiefly humorous, under the titles of "Lapsus calami" and "Quo Musa, tendis?" and each of these met with considerable success. For some time before his death Mr Stephen had been in ill-health, but until quite recently it was thought that he would recover'.

Pall Mall Gazette – 6th February 1892

'Of J.K.S.' by a Cambridge Friend

'During the whole of his time at school, at college and in the world, he stood intellectually a head and shoulders above his fellows. At Eton, the collegers who were his contemporaries, a very brilliant set of men acknowledged 'Jem' Stephen as their chief; others might be clever, but 'Jem' was a genius. At King's he won his fellowship by dissertations on International Law and Political Science, both of which perhaps showed more promise than performance. There were some who complained that his election was off the usual academical lines, but for myself I should have thought a college disgraced who did not receive into her society her most brilliant son. His influence was everywhere. He was the centre of admiration, not only at the Union, but at a dozen other Societies, debating and literary. Nor were his purely social gifts less remarkable. An enthousiastic Etonian, he kept up all his school connections with unabated vigour, and was always at home amongst an Eton circle. We often saw him at Cambridge. The undergraduates admired his great qualities to the full; they treated all his efforts with serious attention; his eccentricities were apparently unnoticed, certainly unreproved by them. In our midst he grew every day better and more himself. He repaid us bountifully.'

St James's Gazette – 6th February 1892

'The Literary World
Literature has sustained a loss-a loss both of performance and promise-in the early death of poor "J K S". What he had done was something; for though we have plenty of minor poets about, we have not so many good vers de societe writers that we can lightly spare the brilliant epigrammatist of "Lapsus Calami". But all those who knew him are agreed that this volume, clever as it was, was no true measure of his powers. He amused himself with Calverley and light literature; but his studies had been in the school of Sir Henry Maine, De Tocqueville, Taine, and the great American federalists. He might have become a philosophical politician, or a political philosopher, of a kind and stamp such as we do not often grow in England nowadays. Unlike some students of such subjects, he was a man with the keenest sense of style. If he had lived to write the great book his Cambridge friends expected of him, it would assuredly have been a work of literature.'

St James' Gazette – 8th February 1892

'In Memory of J K S
"Quo, Musa, Tendis?"

By the dim paths of earthly fate,
Thy poet soul did tend,
To where before thee lay the gate
Of thy mysterious Friend

Love opened wide the shadowy door –
Love, who had guided thee;
"Enter, dear Soul, thy suffering o'er
From thy tired self set free"

But we who travel yet behind
And toil these paths along,
May mourn the heart so loving kind,
The graceful, friendly song.

Through the great sound of hopes and fears,
Still in thy light verse rings
The careless joy of Eton years,
The merry zest of King's

Sweet vanished hours! Undying yet
In memory's inmost cell,
When we forget them we'll forget
Thee, dearest Jem, as well.'

B H H (Bernard H Holland)

The New York Times – 8th February 1892

'A despatch from London announces the death of J K Stephen, son of Sir James Fitzjames Stephen the magistrate, who presided at the trial of Mrs Maybrick. He was at one time a tutor to the late Duke of Clarence and Avondale at Cambridge. On one occasion he issued a most curious address to the electors of Kilkenny. Serious doubts as to his mental condition were entertained at one time. His best known volume is a poetical work entitled 'Lapsus Calami'.'

Note: The address to the electors of Kilkenny, the traditional centre of Irish Nationalism, was contained in his poem 'An Election Address Dec 1890'. It seems to take to task, in somewhat extreme language, both the British and the Irish factions.

Cambridge Review – 11th February 1892

'In Memoriam J K S' by Walter Headlam

It was here, was it not,
That we wandered, two friends and I,
Past the end of June, when a large half-moon
Sailed sad in a sober sky…..*

Hardly half a year gone by,
Past the end of June
Wandered here two friends and I,
While a silent moon
Mounted in a sober sky

Now, when scarce afresh we see
Flowers upon the earth,
Two are mourners of the three;
Blasted ere their birth
Are the flowers that were to be.

Still for others be the praise
Of the matchless tongue
While for me one memory stays
Treasured most among
My remembered garden-days.'

*Lines taken from JKS's own poem 'In a Garden' published in Lapsus Calami.

The 'two friends and I' refer to Walter Headlam, Edward Benson and Stephen.

The Speaker - 13 February 1892 (Extract)

'Mr J K Stephen has died, and a most striking personality is lost to Cambridge. A genial companion, a witty conversationalist, and an eloquent speaker, the author of "Lapsus Calami" was never a man to pass unnoticed among his fellows. His "Reflector", his threatened descent upon Kilkenny, and, finally, his lively "slips of the pen," brought him before the public.

He presented himself as "a pupil of C S C," but the expression does not define him. He was something less, and something more. We are reminded most distinctly of Calverley in the "Lines at the Riverside." The poet comes upon a "shawl on the grass," by the river's brink, and pictures to himself the fate of the wearer – a suicide:

> "Doubt, hesitation, and fear,
> Madness, delusion, despair,
> All of them culminate there,
> There by the swift-rushing weir,"

And so the description continues until it is broken in upon by the real possessor of the inspiring rag:

> "Only a nursery-maid
> Come back to look for her shawl"

Endings like this abound in Calverley. It was a favourite stage-trick of his which may be imitated with success.

The parodies in "Lapsus Calami" of F W H Myers, Wordsworth, and Walt Whitman (we arrange according to the merit of the "sincere flatteries") have also a flavour of the master. They tickle one's ear with the rhythms of the poets imitated, and one's sense of humour with the absurdity of the thoughts expressed. They are quiet, confident, and flowing.

But while J K S is not so finished an artist as C S C, he has, at any rate, published attempts of much more varied nature than his beloved master.

We find another mood in "Quo Musa Tendis" which is absent in Calverley, the mood of cynicism. "A Remonstrance," "A Joke," "An After-thought," "After the Golden Wedding," and "A Pair of Fools" are all bitter, like the following portrait:-

> "Oh yes! I know the sort of man!
> A not entirely vacant eye;
> A ready smile, a kind of style;
> A forehead adequately high;
> Curls more or less Olympian.
>
> The type is common: wherefore tarry
> To paint what all must know so well?
> He's rather tall, his feet are small,
> He's thoroughly conventional:
> A man who moves in common grooves,
> And never startles you at all;
> Or, all in one sad phrase to tell,
> The sort of man that women marry."

West London Reporter – 13th February 1892 (Extract)

'Mr J K Stephen, whose early death has cut short a singularly promising career, proved himself from his earliest years the possessor of exceptionally brilliant talents. During his schooldays at Eton he shewed much aptitude for the composition of humorous verse, and some of his contributions to the Eton Chronicle are remembered and quoted by succeeding generations of Eton boys. At Cambridge he carried everything before him in the department of law and history. He shone, moreover, as an able public speaker, and was elected President of the Union. Subsequently he returned to a London sphere, and presented the public with two volumes of verse, which attracted a good deal of attention by their neatness and felicity. The first was entitled "Lapsus Calami," and the second, published a few weeks ago, "Quo Musa, Tendis?" both written somewhat after the Calverly manner.'

The Granta – February 13th 1892

'J K STEPHEN
(Died Feb 3rd, 1892)

Untimely loss! Ah, melancholy phrase,
Sad as the echo of the passing bell.
Untimely lost, yet not too soon for praise,
Dear friend and fellow-worker, fare you well.

You sleep, and sleep, I think, you most desired:
Your spirit could not brook the dragging chain:
Beaten against the bars, and bruised, it tired,
And longed for rest when life had turned to pain.

Yet we who loved you fain had kept you here,
Here mid the spacious courts you loved to pace
Here mid the grey old walls you held so dear,
Where youth and hope revived you for a space.

Oft did I meet you by our winding Cam,
Talked, jested, argued while we sat and dined;
Heard you in scorn of many a loud-voiced sham,
Speak homely sense in brilliant words enscrined.

And oft in fancy did I wreathe your name
With praise and honour, won by strength and skill;
Beheld you climb the steep that leads to fame,
And watched you ever rising higher still.

Till all was yours on which your heart was set:
And now – the Curtain closes on the scene;
And sorrow claims us, and a vain regret
For all we lose, and all that might have been.

Oft shall we pause upon our daily round,
And one shall mourning to the other say,
"Here did his joyous, kindly welcome sound,"
Or "here he sudden flashed from grave to gay."

Or "here he rolled sonorous eloquence,
With magic sentences enthralled the ear,
Till just the one word, squared to fit the sense,
Dropped to its place and made his meaning clear".

Or "here he thrilled us with swift-darting shocks
Of lightning humour, or with innocent guile
O'erturned our arguments with paradox,
And lulled our reason with that glowing smile."

Never again: the thin-spun life is slit,
The bright-hued, lambent flame expires in gloom,
Whither, we questioned, tends the Muse of wit?
Comes the dread answer-to the silent tomb.

Oh massive head that great thoughts seemed to bow,
Oh lustrous eyes whose light we ill could spare,
Oh genial face, and noble, classic brow
Broad 'neath its tangled mass of heavy hair,

Farewell, farewell; not wholly are ye gone;
Something we keep, though much we loved departs.
For while we live your memory lives on,
Deathless, dear friend, dear Jem, within our hearts.'

TIS

The Bookman – March 1892 (Extract)

'From the first he was beloved and admired by his contemporaries and was regarded as a genius from the sense of power, which he diffused. Undoubtedly the most brilliant year of Stephen's life was his last. He arrived in Cambridge in November 1890, and became at once the darling and the wonder of the under-graduates. Eccentric as he was in his dress, and in some of his habits, his eloquence was never more powerful, his judgement in the affairs of others never more sound. He was equally popular in town and university, with men and women. No one knew whether to admire or to love him most. He was one of the best and most gifted spirits whom they had ever known.'

Oscar Browning

Cambridge Review – March 1893

' "Anniversary" by Walter Headlam (Extract)

My thought comes true:
When the kin dust upon the dust they threw
And *"Death!"* was echoed from that earthy scene,
Yet well I knew,
Even at that hour, that ere his grave were green
Sorrow would hurt me with an edge less keen;
And now I find the pain has past away
In part, and I can say
"This was once, but is over, and has been,
By waning with each day" :

A marvel rare
Beyond the range of human hearts it were
If to that saving trust they should not cleave,
That no despair
Need gloom for loss no morrow may retrieve,
Because Death cannot endlessly bereave,
But they shall meet upon some further shore,
Not to be parted more:-
Whatever utmost fancies Hope may weave
Of what Death has in store,
None ever yet so dear she wove
As lost ones to be loved hereafter and to love.

I will not strive
Desperately out of blankness to revive
My one-time ravishing but forgotten strain,
Nor keep alive
The vanished rainbow at such cost of pain;
Though I may never capture them again,

> Once loved, not uneffectually have they
> Past from my sense away,
> But undiscerned their influences remain
> That shall not so decay:-
> Nor am I traitor to my friend
> Because I weep no more, if so my weeping end.'

The Academy – 19 August 1905 (Extract)

'No literary reputations are so short-lived as those of the parodists. But since Calverley, who has been dead these ever so many years, is still read and quoted, one may hope that the memory and the works of J K S will survive the passing of the generation that knew and loved him. In parody he broke away from Calverley and, as some are inclined to say, excelled him. The contrast between, for instance, his 'The Last Ride Together' and Calverley's 'The Cock and the Bull' is enough to show the difference in treatment; it is perhaps a difference between parodying matter and parodying form.

His memory must be very dear and very precious, the memory of a brilliant, a too brilliant, man, witty, charming and full of a feverish virility. 'It may be worthwhile' said his brother 'to remind those who know him only as the author of Lapsus Calami, and Quo Musa Tendis? that those works represent only a small and comparatively trifling part of his talents, and give no indication of the features of his character best remembered by those who knew him with any degree of intimacy'.

The Times Literary Supplement – 31 January 1942 (Extract)

'There are many to whom the term "light verse" conjures up exclusively the names of a handful of nineteenth-century poets, of whom Hood, Praed, and Calverley were the chief. The popularity of these writers in Victorian days makes this excusable, but it is none the less a mistake. When Mr W H Auden put together "The Oxford Book of Light Verse" a few years ago he wisely stretched his net so as to include not only the work of Chaucer and Skelton, but also that of Belloc and Chesterton, as well as a rather generous selection of bits and pieces by anonymous writers. The anthology confirmed what is surely the true view of his delightful art – that it is something sui generis, never comparable to (or indeed desiring comparison with) serious poetry, but in which success is equally difficult and equally rare.

Yet there were strange omissions in Mr Auden's book. If the connoisseur was surprised at being deprived of Thackeray, he was still more pained to find that he was given nothing by J K Stephen. Unable to believe that the author of "Lapsus Calami" had been left out on purpose, he wondered whether he had been forgotten. The fiftieth anniversary of the death of this well-loved and remarkably gifted young man, however, gives an opportunity of keeping his fame alive among a different and less fortunate generation than his own. No lover of light verse would wish to see that opportunity neglected.

Like his predecessor, Winthrop Praed, with whom he had much in common, he was one who loved his time at Eton and never ceased to be grateful for it.

His poem on "The Old School List" is an intellectual advance on Praed's "School and Schoolfellows," and has the dignity of true sentiment.

Considering that J K Stephen's verses were only the casual by-products of a mind that was always intensely absorbed in the problems of scholarship, of law and of politics, and in the daily society of friends who delighted in the brilliance of his talk, the hundred or so poems that he left behind him were not an ungenerous allowance. They had, moreover, a uniform excellence rare to a general collection. Perhaps his best work was done in parody (Browning being the chief sufferer); but he was not merely, or even primarily, a parodist. Nor – though he wrote of "all the harm that women have done," and in "Cynicus to W Shakspere" declared:-

> You wrote a line too much, my sage,
> Of seers the first, and first of sayers;
> For only half the world's a stage,
> And only all the women players

was he a misogynist. His generous nature made amends to Browning in "A Parodist's Apology," and to the ladies in several of his later poems; the truth, according to A C Benson, is that he had "a very emotional nature combined with a horror of sentimental situations."

The admirer and follower of Praed and Calverley, though he had their gift of mingling humour with pathos, owed less to their inspiration than might have been imagined. His success lay largely in his restraint and in the simplicity of an original style. Who in re-reading the teetotal "Drinking Song." The "Elegy on De Marsay," the wistful "Blue Hills," or "The Dawn of the Year," could imagine them better done? Yet his verses-though they hint at it-cannot quite explain the hold that J K Stephen obtained over the hearts and minds of his contemporaries. Much that lies within the charm of a personality cannot, in default of a Boswell, be retrieved for posterity. At least let us guard what trace remains of that magic-and be thankful that we can still take "Lapsus Calami" down from the shelf, fifty years after.'

The Times – 3 February 1942 (Extract)

'J K S

There are many who can still remember the excitement caused in the year 1891 by the publication at Cambridge of two slim little books of verse called "Lapsus Calami" and "Quo Musa Tendis?" There are also some (but a small and ever-lessening band) who can remember hearing words of wit and wisdom flow from the lips of James Kenneth Stephen, the author of those little books-and they especially will not have forgotten the shock of his untimely death, just fifty years ago today.

Wherever else he is forgotten, J K Stephen, like W M Praed, will always be remembered at Eton and Cambridge. Praed , in his inimitable way, voiced the sentimental yearning of the Old Etonian of the eighteen-twenties:-

> Where are my friends? I am alone;
> No playmate shares my beaker:
> Some lie beneath the churchyard stone,
> And some-before the Speaker

And Stephen fifty years later took up the same theme:-

> There are some who did nothing at school much since
> And others much then, since naught:
> They are middle-aged men, grown bald since then:
> Some have travelled, and some have fought:
> And some have written, and some are bitten

With strange new faiths: desist
From tracking them: broker or priest or prince.
They are all in the old School List.

Cambridge men were quick to see in him the lineal descendant of C S Calverley, and Stephen was quick to acknowledge the debt:-

If any critic would remark in fine
"Of C S C, this gentle art he learned"
I should not then expect my book to fail,
Nor have my doubts about a decent sale.

J K S was more than the representative of "the eternal undergraduate" within us who "rejoices before life". There was in him a strength and virility of character contrasting with the delicacy of his art and finding expression in one of his stanzas quoted this morning as "Old and True" – something which suggests that, if the fates had set him down at the present crisis of our existence he would have been equal to the occasion.'

ii. Medical Reports

a) This is the paper written by Stephen in May 1891 in response to Dr George Savage's letter dated 21 November 1890 (Stephen writes of himself in the third person).

'Private and Confidential

About the end of October last Dr G H Savage, of 3, Henrietta Street, formerly Principal of Bedlam, formed the opinion that the gentleman hereinafter referred to was not in a state of perfect mental health, but was suffering from morbid excitement or cerebral exaltation. Dr Savage had some personal acquaintance with the gentleman in question and his past career, but the opinion in question was formed without personal examination, and indeed without seeing the patient.

The opinion of Dr Savage became known to many relations, friends and acquaintances of the object of his suspicion, and to the members of his club, with results of a damaging, if not disastrous character.

The gentleman was never medically examined by Dr Savage; but he was separately examined by Sir Andrew Clark, Dr Hughlings Jackson and Dr Hack Tuke in October, November and December.

Sir Andrew Clark declared that he was in perfect physical health, and would continue so if he adopted certain regulations as to diet, clothing, &c., which he practically did.

Dr Hughlings Jackson was of opinion that his nervous system was in perfect order; he would give no opinion as to his brain.

Dr Hack Tuke, after a very prolonged and minute examination, could find no trace of brain disease; but was of opinion that Dr Savage was unlikely to go wrong on such a matter.

Early in January, 1891, the patient was examined at Paris by two eminent French doctors, who certified in writing that he was free from brain disease.

In December Dr Savage expressed the opinion that the patient ought to be put under restraint; and that, failing this, he ought to go to some quiet and distant place for several months, if possible under the close superintendence of a medical attendant. If this were not done he anticipated an outbreak of a serious, and probably violent, character. He especially deprecated staying in London, visiting Paris, or going to Cambridge.

In defiance of Dr Savage's advice his patient stayed in London, visited Paris, and went to Cambridge.

No serious or violent attack took place.

Dr Savage's patient had been, since January, at Cambridge and London. In the former place he had lived a busy and active life, seeing old friends, and making new ones; dispensing and receiving hospitality; reading, writing, speaking at public debates and political meetings, lecturing on law and coaching in history. He has contributed to newspapers, begun two books, and published a third. He has taken no advice, and subjected himself to no restraint.

During this time he has corresponded with Dr Savage, and has seen him when in London. At an interview in February

Dr Savage expressed the opinion that he was much better, if not entirely recovered (despite his neglect of advice). Subsequently, after consultation with a friend of both parties resident at Cambridge, Dr Savage and Dr Hack Tuke wrote a joint opinion advising him to stay at Cambridge and go on with his work as a teacher.

In April Dr Savage, at an interview, admitted that his expectations had not come true; and that the defiance of his advice had not produced the expected evils. Upon the patient declaring that he believed he had never suffered from excitement or exaltation, or done anything he had cause to regret. Dr Savage said that this belief was a symptom of dormant disease, and a proof that the recovery was not perfect.

In November, 1890, Dr Savage wrote the following letter, which was sealed up and endorsed "not to be opened till May 1891." On the first of May the patient opened the letter, which ran as follows:

> 3, Henrietta Street
> Cavendish Square, W.
> November 21, 1890

Dear

According to promise I write my opinion as to the next 6 months of your life.

For some weeks to come there will be a waste of money, buying useless things i.e. things for which you have no real need.

You will borrow money right and left. You will dress in unconventional ways and cause worry to your relations.

You will discover that you have incurred debts which of yourself you cannot pay and will feel it a grievance that you have to fall in with conditions which are imposed.

You will then take to bed and spend much of the spring in reading in bed and doing nothing of any good, not earning a living. The period will be one rather of exhaustion than of depression, and so the circle will be completed.

I am,
Yours truly
G.H. SAVAGE

During the first weeks above referred to, the patient bought nothing, borrowed nothing, and dressed conventionally. During the whole of the six months he rose early, worked hard, and earned a fair income. He never made any discovery of debts, which he could not pay.

Dr Savage has often expressed the opinion that his patient would not recover without first going through a prolonged period of depression or exhaustion. It is common ground between him and the patient that no such period has taken place.

Dr Savage says that, owing to peculiar circumstances for which he did not make allowance, his prophecy was not fulfilled: but he declares that his patient's present good health is temporary and that the prophecy will be fulfilled some day.

Dr Savage's opinions as to the future course of the disease were expressed, in November, in unqualified terms and with unbounded confidence.

Under these circumstances it is submitted that the opinion of Dr Savage on this case is absolutely worthless: and that there is no ground to suppose that the person referred to ever suffered from morbid excitement or exaltation.

This suggestion is made, in the interest of a person who has been gravely prejudiced, if not irreparably damaged, by an opinion formed in good faith, but, as he believes, on wholly erroneous grounds. It is not intended to depreciate Dr Savage's deservedly high reputation: but merely to imply that he has, in this case, made one of those mistakes from which the most eminent physicians cannot be wholly exempt.

Cambridge,
May 1891'

b) This is the transcript of pages 172, 173 and 174 of the medical records book of St Andrew's Hospital, Northampton. It covers matters relating to Stephen from his admittance on 21 November 1891 to his death on 3 February 1892

'Stephen, James Kenneth

Admitted November 21st 1891. Age 32 yrs & V mos. Single. Barrister at Law. Church of England. 18 Trinity St. Cambridge. First decided attack (but said to have been suffering from disease affecting mind since 1888). Never under treatment. Duration 24 hours. Supposed cause blow on head in January 1887. Not epileptic. Doubtful whether suicidal. Doubtful whether dangerous. No near relative afflicted with insanity. Usual Medical Attendant: Lawrence Humphrey M.D., 3 Trinity St. Cambridge.

Notice of death to brother (who signs order) Herbert Stephen. 32 DeVere Gardens, Kensington, London W.

MEDICAL STATEMENT:-

Extreme depression-often declining to speak or answer questions. This morning I found him standing naked in his bedroom, smiling. All the furniture & clothes in disorder & in the street were the fragments of looking glass which he had thrown from the window. He has had attacks of depression lasting for some months, followed by periods of unusual excitability: communicated by Harry Lushington Stephen, 32 DeVere Gardens, London, Barrister at Law. This morning in an attack of violence he threw his looking glass out of the window into the street & stood naked in his room & declined to move. Was under a delusion that there was a warrant out for his detention.

Lawrence Humphrey M.D.

STATE ON ADMISSION:-

He is tall, well-built & muscular, in good condition (inclined to be stout). There are no signs of recent disease or injury. Features regular. Eyes blue. Pupils equal, reaction to light normal. Complexion sallow. Hair dark brown, thin on crown of head. Face clean shaven. No organic disease of heart. Lungs sound. Abdominal organs apparently healthy. Tongue clean. Teeth somewhat defective. Pulse 104.

He arrived late at night & soon after admission went to his bath. At first he objected to bathe before "such a crowd"-myself & two attendants-& was somewhat slow & hesitating in undressing. Stated that there was nothing the matter with him except that he suffered from constiptation & that opium was given to relieve this, but that it made him worse. Further than this he would say nothing & went to bed quietly, No 5. C.O. Stanwell.

November 22nd: His brother (Mr. Harry L. Stephen) spent the day with him. He was reserved, taciturn and almost silent all day, at times answering "Yes or No" to questions & at other times not speaking at all. He took a small amount of food at each meal. He spent all his time wandering about the garden or up & down his sitting room & would not read or occupy himself in any way. At bedtime he obstinately refused to go to bed & when an attempt was made to undress him he struck out at the attendant & had to be undressed & put to bed. When once in bed he was perfectly quiet. He was reported to have passed a quiet night & to have slept well. He was up this morning to breakfast with his brother. C.O. Stanwell.

November 23rd. He was yesterday visited by Messrs. Percival & Milligan, whose certificates are copied below; & today by Mr. Wim. Coulson, a Justice for the Borough of Northampton.

MEDICAL STATEMENTS:-

Very depressed, wanders disorderly about & will not amuse nor interest himself in anything. Obstinately refuses to answer any questions or to enter into conversation. His brother (Harry Lushington Stephen, Barrister, 32 DeVere Gardens, London W.) informs me: that he has delusions that there is a plot against him to deprive him of his liberty, that he made an indecent public speech & that he has committed some crime. He was sent for to Cambridge yesterday to see his brother, who had been in a violent state of excitement & destroyed his furniture & clothes, of which things that patient was afterwards unconscious.

G.H. Percival, M.B.

He appears to be very depressed: he absolutely refused to say a word to me & either sits staring moodily into the fire or walks up & down the room paying no attention to anything.

By his brother, Harry Lushington Stephen, 32 deVere Gardens, London W. Barrister. He informs me that his brother has for three years been subject to attacks & loss of self-control, followed by fits of depression & inaction. Yesterday at Cambridge he had an attack of mania, threw some of the furniture out of the room & stood naked for some time in a state of stupor. He has delusions that there is a plot to accuse him of a crime & that he made an indecent public speech.

Robert Arthur Milligan

November 25th: He is reported to have been quiet & to have slept well each night. He has had no action of the bowels since admission & on the 23rd refused to take any medicine, when threatened with the tube he took two pills (Hyd. Colsc. & Hyoscy:) followed after an interval by a dose of house mixture, this has had no effect & this afternoon he had an enema with only slight effect. His appetite is not good. He is reserved & taciturn, occasionally he will answer "Yes or No" but frequently will not speak.

C.O. Stanwell

December 2nd: He is quiet, very reserved, well conducted & giving no trouble. He takes exercise daily in the grounds & garden & when indoors spends all his time in his room reading. He is very quiet at night & reported to sleep well. He has a very fair appetite & is in good bodily health, though his bowels act very irregularly. He gives expression to no delusion & seldom says more than "Yes or No."

C.O. Stanwell.

December 9th: Still reserved & quiet. Sits by himself all day when indoors usually reading. Quiet & giving no trouble. Seldom says more than "Yes or No" but appears to be comfortable & contented. Appetite good & in good bodily health.

C.O. Stanwell.

December 16th: Very reserved and unsociable, though somewhat more cheerful. Reads a great deal. Takes country walks with his attendant. Apparently contented & giving no trouble. Seldom gets up in the morning till his breakfast is ready. Troubled a good deal with constipation, otherwise in good health.

C.O. Stanwell.

December 23rd: He is unnaturally reserved, but more cheerful & apparently contented. Will not take part in any amusement. Keeps entirely to himself & takes exercise in the country. His appetite is good & he is in good bodily health. Suffers somewhat from constipation & requires aperient medicine about twice a week.

C.O. Stanwell.

1892 January 13th: Since last note he continued to improve, was more cheerful & sociable, playing billiards & taking regular exercise outside until the 10th. On the 9th he was visited by Lady Stephen & since then he has been very reserved & irritable. His appetite is poor, he will not go out, he reads very little, whereas before he used to read a great deal, he spends most of his time pacing up & down his room with his hands in his pockets. Frequently he will not answer a question. His bowels do not act at all regularly & tonight he threw two pills into the fire. This evening he would not allow his fire to be made up though the night is cold, & kept two windows in his room open. Except for the constipation he is in good bodily health.

C.O. Stanwell.

January 18th: For the last three days he has taken no food & has been fed three times each day with a feeding tube. Yesterday & today he has struggled so violently that it is impossible to feed him by the mouth for fear of breaking his teeth when resisting to have the mouth open, that he has been fed through the nose. Aperient medicine has been given but as this had no effect, today he had an enema with a fairly good result. He has been very violent to the attendants. He seldom speaks a word. Frequently out of bed standing on the floor or sitting on the edge of his bed. He was yesterday transferred to a warm room in the Infirmary from 4a where he had been in bed for three days.

C.O. Stanwell.

January 21st: He is still refusing his food & is fed three times with the nasal tube. There has been no action of the bowels since the morning of the 18th after an enema. On external examination a collection of hard masses of faecal matter was found & this morning another enema was given & several large masses came away. When fed this afternoon a draught containing Tinct. Rhei, Dec Aloes Co. & Tinct. Belladon was given, but at present has had no effect. He passes water in bed & while sitting in the chair for feeding & will not use the chamber utensil. Three letters have come for him from Lady Stephen (one yesterday & two today) but he will not open them. He offers little or no resistance before feeding but always tries to prevent the tube from passing by shaking his head & occasionally by coughing it into his mouth. Temperature 98.2. Pulse 96 & fairly good.

C.O. Stanwell.

January 30th: He is still refusing his food & is being fed three times a day with the nasal tube. He has drunk one cup of tea & half a cup of coffee, but cannot be induced to take more. His strength is well maintained.

C.O. Stanwell.

February 2nd: Yesterday & the day before he sucked the juice from an orange & today he has swallowed a very small quantity of brandy & water. Yesterday he suddenly became very much collapsed with a feeble pulse 123 & anxious expression, skin very dry, temp: 98 degrees. Today he is very feeble, tongue dry & he swallows a small quantity of cold water with great difficulty. He has been fed daily 2 eggs, half pint milk & 2oz Brandy morning and night and strong beef tea ½ pint, 2 eggs & 2oz Port midday. Last night he had in addition to the eggs and milk a small teaspoonful of Liebigs extract of meat. At the midday feed today he vomited more than half back & was very much exhausted. This evening he has had one egg, 5oz milk & 3 oz Brandy through the tube & has since been slightly better. His mouth has been washed out with weak Condy's fluid. The bowels have been acting fairly regularly lately & were open today, owning to small doses of Ext. Cascara Sagrada given night & morning. He has been very quiet & sleeps for a short time at intervals both night & day.

C.O. Stanwell.

February 3rd: During last night he took a fair amount of nourishment: jelly, beeftea, 1 egg & brandy, though he swallowed with great difficulty. He frequently remarked "It's too late," when the feeding cup was put to his lips. He was visited by two brothers at 2 A.M. & talked to them. He remained conscious to within two hours of his death. At two thirty he became unconscious & sank rapidly. He died at 4.22

PM in the presence of his Mother (Lady Stephen), two brothers, myself & the Chief Attendant.

C.O. Stanwell.

STATEMENT OF THE CAUSE OF DEATH.

James Kenneth Stephen died on the 3rd day of February 1892 at 4.22 P.M. in the presence of Edwin Cave, Chief Attendant. The cause of death being: - Mania, Refusal of food, Exhaustion.

Signed J. BAYLEY
Medical Superintendent'

Bibliography

Abrahamsen, David, *Murder and Madness* (London, Robson Books 1992).

Amis, Kingsley, *The New Oxford Book of Light Verse* (Oxford, Oxford University Press 1978).

Anderson, Garrett, *A History of the Savile Club* (London, Savile Club 1993).

Annan, Noel, *Leslie Stephen. The Godless Victorian* (London, Weidenfeld and Nicolson 1984).

Aronson, Theo, *Prince Eddy and the Homosexual Underworld* (London, John Murray 1994).

Bell, Quentin, *Virginia Woolf* (London, Hogarth Press, 1972).

Benson, A C, *The Leaves on the Tree* (London, Smith Elder 1911).

Briggs, Julie, *Virginia Woolf – An Inner Life* (London, Allen Lane, 2005).

Browning, Oscar, *Memories of Sixty Years* (London, The Bodley Head, 1910).

Cole, Maurice, *Thorpe Mandeville History of the Parish* (–, –, 1996).

Connell, John, *W. E. Henley* (London, Constable 1949).

Cook, Andrew, *Prince Eddy, The King Britain Never Had* (Stroud, Tempus, 2006).

Cox, Michael, *M R James. An Informal Portrait* (Oxford, Oxford University Press 1983).

Croome, A C M, *Fifty Years of Sport* (London, Walter Southwood 1913).

Deacon, Richard, *The Cambridge Apostles* (London, Robert Royce, 1985).

Ellman, Richard, *Oscar Wilde* (London, Hamish Hamilton, 1987).

Fairclough, Melvyn, *The Ripper and the Royals* (London, Gerald Duckworth, 1991).

Gayford, Martin, *The Yellow House* (London, Penguin 2006).

Gimson, Andrew, *The Rise of Boris Johnson* (London, Simon & Schuster, 2006).

Harrison, Michael, *Clarence* (New York, Drake, 1974).

Hart-Davis, Rupert, *The Letters of Oscar Wilde* (London, Hart-Davis, 1962).

Headlam, Cecil, *Life and Letters of Walter Headlam* (London, Duckworth, 1910).

James, M R, *Eton and King's* (London, Williams and Norgate 1926).

Johnson, Michael, *A History of Outwood* (Redhill, Outwood Local History 1997).

Kaplan, Fred, *Henry James – The Imagination of Genius* (London, Hodder and Stoughton 1992).

King, James, *Virginia Woolf* (London, Hamish Hamilton, 1994).

Longford, Elizabeth, *Victoria R I* (London, Weidenfeld and Nicolson, 1964).

Lowe, Gill, *Hyde Park Gate News* (London, Hesperus Press, 2005).

Lubenow, W C, *The Cambridge Apostles* (Cambridge, Cambridge University Press, 1998).

MacCarthy, Desmond, *Portraits* (London, Putnam 1931).

Macnaghten, Hugh, *Fifty Years of Eton* (London, George Allen & Unwin, 1924).

McDonald, Deborah, *The Prince, his tutor, and the Ripper* (U.S.A. McFarland, 2007).

Maitland, F W, *Life and Letters of Leslie Stephen* (London, Duckworth, 1906).

Masters, Brian, *The Life of E F Benson* (London, Chatto and Windus, 1991).

Morley, Sheridan, *Oscar Wilde* (London, Weidenfeld and Nicolson, 1976).

Nicolson, Harold, *George V* (London, Constable, 1952)

O'Donnell, Kevin, *Jack the Ripper Whitechapel Murders* (St Osyth, Ten Bells, 1997).

Palmer, Geoffrey and Lloyd, Noel, *EF Benson – As He Was* (Luton, Lennard Publishing, 1988).

Pearsall, Ronald, *The Worm in the Bud* (London, Weidenfeld and Nicolson, 1969)

Pfaff, Richard William, *Montague Rhodes James* (London, Scolar Press, 1980).

Plumb, J H, *Studies in Social History* (London, Longmans 1955).

Ricks, Christopher, *The New Oxford Book of Victorian Verse* (Oxford, Oxford University Press 1987).

Rose, Kenneth, *Superior Person* (London, Weidenfeld and Nicolson, 1969).

Stephen, Leslie, *Life of Sir James Fitzjames Stephen* (London, Smith and Elder 1895).

Vincent, James, *The Duke of Clarence* (London, John Murray 1893).

Weintraub, Stanley, *Edward, King in Waiting* (London, John Murray 2000).

Index